*Messages on Mission from a man who lived—* **In**
# Stride
*with* **God**

### Selections from the letters, lectures, sermons and articles of Paul J. Lindell

### Edited by Anders B. Hanson

**WORLD MISSION PRAYER LEAGUE**
Minneapolis, Minnesota

IN STRIDE WITH GOD
Copyright © 1987 World Mission Prayer League

PRINTED IN THE UNITED STATES OF AMERICA

# Contents

# Foreword

*"There is a tide in the affairs of men which taken at the flood, leads on to fortune. Omitted, and all the voyage of their life is bound in shallows and misery." (From Julius Caesar, Act IV, by William Shakespeare)*

*"And who knows, whether you have not come to the kingdom for such a time as this?" Esther 4:14b*

Paul Lindell was a unique channel of God's grace and blessing for thousands.  Some of the streams of lively, godly influence which poured into his life, nourishing, shaping and preparing him for that ministry are revealed in these collected papers.

An early strain of such vigorous spiritual influence was the life, love, godly example and faithful service of Paul's missionary parents, John and Selma Lindell. The Lindells were missionaries to China under the Augustana Lutheran Church. Pastor Lindell died early in a typhus epidemic while deeply engaged in his evangelistic task, leaving three young sons, Paul, Jonathan and David. Mother Lindell's faith, courage and commitment to Christ held the family together and left the mark of faith, love and grace on Paul and his brothers.

Another stream of divine grace flowed into Paul's life through the church in China, quickened, renewed, revived by a deep cleansing movement of the Holy Spirit.  Paul often spoke and wrote with joy and gratitude of the powerful, life-changing impact the Chinese Church in revival had made on his life as a high-school lad.

Paul was exposed to the range and breadth of variety found in the many denominations of the Christian church during his China boyhood.  He carried with him through the years a

5

healthy appreciation for Christians of differing backgrounds and convictions. However, he knew not only by background, family, church and school that he must be Lutheran, but also through study, reflection and personal conviction. Again and again he spoke of his personal debt to, and gratitude for the Lutheran Church, a church of the Bible, rooted in sound, evangelical doctrine, giving rise to a robust, winsome piety in daily life.

The stream of the evangelical missionary movement was also deeply influential in Paul's life. The 19th Century was described by that incomparable historian of world mission, Kenneth Scott Latourette, as "the great century" in world mission. Paul Lindell drew heavily on the movements, pioneers, and purposes of that stream of mission for his own life's vision and purpose. He eloquently transmitted those histories, visions, and purpose to a new generation of 20th Century missionary candidates and supporters. The accounts of William Carey, Hudson Taylor, Robert Morrison, Amy Carmichael, C. T. Studd and many others, pioneers of both church and interdenominational missionary societies, fueled the fires of missionary vision and challenge which, ignited in his heart, served in turn to enflame the hearts and stir the minds of hundreds of young people.

Those who had the privilege of knowing and working with Paul—friend, brother, exemplar in faith and leader in mission—felt he was God's man for world mission in the mid 20th Century, "come to the kingdom for such a time as this."

And Paul himself—with genuine reluctance and humility—recognized and surrendered himself to be such a leader in Lutheran circles, in sounding the call to world mission. But just as important to him was the intense conviction that a "tide of the Spirit" was moving in the world of men. Such signs of a new tide of life and stirring in the world were: the breakup of colonialism in the third world, the drawing together of people in "the global village," the new technologies bringing ease of travel and communication, the new mobility following World War II of people in the western countries, the hundreds of young people restless and ready for the ultimate challenge of missionary service. All of these constituted a tide in the affairs of men upon which Paul Lindell was determined to sail and to carry many with him on that exciting voyage to evangelize the world for Christ.

What about the character of the man? He was:

* A man of zeal, tempered with genuine appreciation of and love for persons.
* A man of prayer and faith, bound in union with Christ his Lord, intoxicated by the life of the Spirit.
* A man of generosity and largeness of heart in relationships with people. Young and old alike found that he was genuinely interested in them as persons. And this trait gained him an entee into the heart and experience of North Americans, Asians, Latin Americans or Europeans, all of whom felt welcome and at ease with him.
* An eloquent preacher, teacher and writer, but this was not so much a studied art as it was the fruit of his personal passion for Christ and his kingdom cause.
* A devoted father, deeply interested and concerned about the growth of his children in body, mind and spirit.
* A man of compassion and sympathy both broad and deep which flowed from his heart into the deep hurts and sorrows of the people around him. At a time of personal crisis and sorrow in our lives, Paul's letters brought to us genuine consolation and a bracing message of faith in the risen Lord.
* A man of continuing lively curiosity at all the marvels of God's creation, a voracious reader and dedicated student.
* A man ready for, practiced and experienced in the schools of simplicity, sacrifice and suffering. He had grasped the biblical, evangelical truth of a costly, but grace-given discipleship for the sake of Jesus Christ.

A careful reading of the pages that follow will further reveal the life and ministry of this man whom God used to stir and move a generation of young men and women in the church for missionary service to the ends of the earth.

**—Frank Wilcox**

# Introduction

As far as I have been able to ascertain, Paul John Lindell did not write an autobiography nor compile a history of the World Mission Prayer League, much as such volumes would have enriched the annals of missionary lore. However, the readers of this record will be able to meet Paul and catch the spirit of the Mission through selected portions of letters and transcribed sermons, Bible studies and published articles from the pen and mouth of Paul.

During a period of several years following Paul's death, his brother Jonathan together with Paul's wife, Margaret, assembled a sizable amount of Paul's papers. At the invitation of Jonathan—shortly before his untimely death in 1985—I was requested, on the basis of my life-long association with Paul, to assist in selecting and preparing materials for eventual publication. What now appears in this book, *In Stride With God*, is my response to that request and the direction of the World Mission Prayer League Fiftieth Anniversary Committee.

You as readers may find it of some interest and possibly of some help as well to be "walked through" the varied array of items that make up this "anthology." In the time-honored parlance of journalism, let us just say that the selection and arrangement of these various pieces (several of which have been abridged) provide us with the **who, where, when, how, what** and **why** of God's mission as reflected in the life and work of a man named Paul and the Mission he was called to lead.

**Who** was Paul? Part I provides a very brief glimpse of this man whose purpose, yes, whose passion it was to walk in stride with God's plan for his life. Prayer was a basic ingredient in his life and that of the "Prayer League." Evidence of that is found in the central place given to prayerful seeking of God's guidance and prayerful dependence on God's provision in the operation of the Mission.

**Where** would Paul's walk with God take him and the Mission? The vision in which Paul's life was caught up focused to a great extent on the still unevangelized areas of the world, such as the heartlands of South America, Asia and Africa. These areas became the targets of the Mission's thrust as is spelled out in Part II.

**When** did Paul's involvement in WMPL take place? And **how** did the new mission operate? Some of the answers are found in Part III.

**What** kind of a mission and what kinds of missionaries were shaped under Paul's leadership? **What** was the challenge that Paul addressed to the church in terms of its mission responsibility? Part IV gives an insight into the makings of the WMPL enterprise and its personnel.

**Why** was Paul consumed by this missionary commitment? Part V points to a double concern: a renewed and revitalized church in America on the one hand, and also the planting and nurture of the church in heretofore unevangelized regions on earth. To that end God in a mighty way used his servant Paul Lindell both at home and abroad.

It is with the same purpose and in the same spirit that the World Mission Prayer League on the occasion of its fiftieth anniversary has undertaken to publish this book both as a token of its grateful memory of Paul's ministry and as a reminder of its continued commitment to continue "in stride with God."

**—Anders Hanson**

*Minneapolis*
*August 1987*

# 1
# A Man
# In Stride With God

*Paul Lindell, possibly more than any other single person, left his stamp on the life and activity of the World Mission Prayer League. In order to grasp and understand the message of this collection of Paul's sermons and lectures, studies and reports, articles and letters, let us take our place in the audience during the recognition service in early December, 1973, when Paul made his last public appearance among his colleagues, supporters and friends. Listen once again to his words of response to the words of tribute and appreciation expressed on that occasion:*

Few people are given such a glorious privilege as I have this afternoon, and I have been sitting here sensing the great debt I owe in every direction. For all that's taken place during these last thirty-some years since my finishing school and getting into God's work, is not something that somehow has come out of me. It is something that God has set before me and poured into me. I've been an earthen vessel . . . a fragile and a mortal vessel, but God has been pouring and pouring his goodness in all kinds of ways into my life and into my way; and I've had the very, very blessed sense all these years of being on course. All through these years there has been a steady, reassuring sense all the way through that the work we have done, the course we have taken has been a course God has set before us; and I've had no doubts about that, and no troubles in my soul and mind even in times of the greatest testing. . . .

Lately I've had some temptations to doubt, to wonder whether the course will remain steady and firm and the work which has begun can reach its fulfillment. But here again I am thankful that God has shielded and reassured me that "He who began the good work in you will perfect it until the coming of the Lord Jesus Christ."

There are three things I'd like to briefly say. One is a word of thanks to God. . . . I had the great privilege to be born in China of godly parents and there too to grow up in a Chinese congregation and then to go to a mission school. During a winter vacation (when I was in high school) I came to my home church and discovered that people were meeting in the church all day, from morning to late at night, in an unheated church, without program and without announcements and without great speakers, just drawn, called, moved by God's Spirit. . . . There with open Bibles they sought the Lord and the Lord met them. . . .The quickening fire of God's Spirit was so evident and it caught me and my inner soul was turned inside out. And for the first time in my life I began to see and to be greatly burdened by my sins. . . . I shall never cease to thank God for the day when the promise of forgiveness brought me the grace of forgiveness and the burden of my sins was lifted and I had peace with God. I thank God for that. I don't understand it, but oh, I shall never, never cease to praise God that the one thing through all these years that has remained steady is a constant hunger and thirst for Jesus to be my life, my daily bread, my water, my all in all.

The second thing I'd like to say is a word of thanks to all of you and to many others. I am a debtor to you. I am a debtor in the Lutheran Church. I am so thankful I've been in the large family of Lutherans. We've got our troubles . . . our problems . . . our sins, but somehow through it all God has put a deposit in our church of the Bible, and solid, sound doctrine by which millions have walked and lived and died in assured faith. So I've been for seeing Lutherans through the country and through these years find each other, hold hands with each other, pull together and work for unity and for common-ness of faith and purpose, rather than wrangle about differences. . . . I have a debt, a great debt to the Lutheran Church, the Lutheran family.

I want to say a word of gratitude, or debt, to my family, to my dear wife who has stood with me and helped carry the burdens of work and life through these years, and my children, four of them who have given to us the full measure of their life and confidence and trust . . . I am in debt to them and thank God for such children.

Now if I may add just one more thing . . . what lies before me, whether long or short, I don't know . . . but I can see almost every day how bit by bit my strength is ebbing, and yet it may be a long time before God finally takes me; but this afternoon I sense I'm having the last time of my life to say a word of thanks to you and a public word of praise to God, whom I love, and Jesus my Savior and my Lord, who has come and made himself all things to me. Praise His Name! Glory to God!

There is an old song that expresses the feeling I have this afternoon:

> "Come, Thou Fount of Every Blessing,
> Tune my heart to sing Thy praise,
> Streams of mercy never ceasing,
> Call for songs of loudest praise.
> Teach me some melodious sonnet,
> Sung by flaming tongues above,
> Praise the mount, I'm fixed upon it,
> Mount of Thy redeeming love.
>
> Here I raise my Ebenezer,
> Hither by Thy grace I've come,
> And I hope by Thy good pleasure,
> Safely to arrive at Home.
> Jesus sought me when a stranger,
> Wandering from the fold of God,
> He to rescue me from danger,
> Interposed His precious blood.
>
> Oh, to grace how great a debtor,
> Daily I'm constrained to be,
> Let Thy goodness like a fetter,
> Bind my wandering heart to Thee.
> Prone to wander, Lord, I feel it,
> Prone to leave the God I love,
> Here's my heart, O take and seal it,
> Seal it for Thy courts above."

# 2

# A Man Acquainted
# With Pain

*During his last years of life Paul Lindell suffered from
cancer and died at the age of 58. Out of his experience with
his illness came a book titled, **The Mystery of Pain.** In the
penetrating search for an answer to this age-old human
problem, Paul presents a deeply spiritual, biblical and personal testimony to one of life's deepest and most stubborn
mysteries.*

*The following selected passages reveal something of the
searching, struggle and solution that Paul experienced in
coping with his painful illness:*

• There is a mystery about pain, suffering, illness, sorrow,
and death. If all of these were merely a problem, philosophy
or theology could look for an answer. Or, if pain were no more
than a maladjustment of some kind, the medical people, or
the science people could find ways to cure it. But pain,
however it comes, is an event. And that is how the Bible meets
it. It does not give us some neat, logical answer to the puzzle
of pain, for there is none. It is plainly a mystery.

• The power and willingness of Jesus to deliver from pain
is surely unlimited . . . and we know this. But we stand
helpless in the midst of a stricken world that bleeds, and
suffers, and weeps for all the pains that hurt so much. . . . Why

is the gap between God's healing power and our need for healing and deliverance so wide and unbridgeable?

• Health and well-being are derivatives from the first creation . . . the same full health and wholeness will again be realized in the final resurrection, in the new earth . . .

• Meanwhile, between the first creation's beginning and the triumph of the new creation, this wholeness has been disrupted, due to sin. Pain and tragedy come from brokenness, brokenness with God . . . Now for us who live in this interim period between the two creations there come three significant experiences: of the goodness of nature, of pain and of a foretaste of the resurrection.

• And now there remains only one more word. What, after all is said and done, am I to do about pain?. . . For one thing, I will accept pain . . . I will accept as real and actual all the pains of life, those that touch me, those that hurt other people, and those that I see in the creation around me . . . They are there and they hurt. I will be honest with them and will deal with them as realistically as I can. . . . Now, if I accept pain as right for the earth I will accept it as right for me too, since in my body I am of the dust of the earth and thus share in the actual matter and destiny of the old creation.

• The Cross of Jesus demonstrated how God uses pain, loss, evil, and death to bring about good. He took the fiercest attack of Satan and turned it into the instrument of salvation.
Similarly, God has taken some of the worst afflictions that have come into the lives of his people and has turned these into routes of blessing for families, tribes and nations.

• Now the second thing I will do with pain is to tackle it, assail it, lay my hands on it and remove it if at all possible. . . . Therefore I will use the tools and means that God has given us in this old creation for keeping pains in check and for cultivating health, wholeness and well-being.

• It is from my Lord Jesus Christ (particularly at the cross) that I first learn to accept pain. And then I also learn from him to use all the tools I can to heal hurts, remove pain, alleviate sufferings, and lift the burdens of sorrow and woe wherever they may be found. You may say this is contradictory. I say it is a paradox ... Both of its seemingly contradictory terms are verified in Jesus Christ. ... This is a great part of the mystery surrounding pain!

# 3

# A Man Impressed
# With Prayer

*Part of a transcribed talk given by Paul on August 8, 1972, at Camp Wanamingo.*

As a young Christian I was impressed with the place that prayer should have in the life of a believer. We had an evangelist in China who preached this so strongly all over. The motto of his life, he used to tell us, was "No Bible, no breakfast. No prayer, no breakfast." His name was Leland Wang. I learned from him the strong importance of prayer in the life of a Christian. Then when I came to this country to go to college, I ran into Christians here and there who were teaching the same thing. I heard about the Apostle James who had great big patches of horny skin on his knees that resulted from much kneeling in prayer. I read and people pointed out that we should always be praying and always giving thanks to God for everything. I learned that great men of God were men of prayer. Men like George Mueller who gave himself to prayer. Men like "Praying Hyde" in the Punjab before the turn of the century whose name became well known across the world as a great man of prayer. I was told that a good way to pray was to have a prayer list. Monday you prayed for this and Tuesday you prayed for that because as your prayer list grew, you had to divide it up since you couldn't take care of it all in one day.

So I got myself a little notebook and started to make this my practice. I got all kinds of things to pray for. I picked them out of the church paper. When I met people and they would say to me, "Would you pray for my auntie, or my cousin?" I'd write that down. So the whole thing began to build up and it was quite a thing. I went about it reverently and I thought of all my friends in China and prayed for them. I'd sort of pray my way around the world as I remembered all kinds of churches and missions everywhere. Oh, the notebook got big and heavy. I thought, dear me, I'm developing a real prayer life like these other fellows had.

Some people told me how you should really agonize in prayer. I tried to do that. Some people thought it was a great idea to pray all night long. Jesus prayed all night on occasions. I went along on some prayer vigils or whatever they called them. I would start in the evening and I tell you it was a job keeping this thing going all night long until breakfast time in the morning. But I was going to work at this and learn all I could from it.

Then I ran into two ideas that were just a knockout for me. It knocked my little book into a cocked hat and put some dents in me. One thing I began to notice was that in the Scriptures the emphasis that the New Testament puts on the life of God's people is an emphasis upon faith. When God gathered up the whole story of his people in the eleventh chapter of Hebrews, the key to all their accomplishments was faith. That "by faith Moses..." All the outstanding things of his life were by faith. Abraham—the four outstanding points of his life were pivotal events in his life and what determined the course he took was faith. I read such things as: "This is the victory which over-comes the world, even your faith," "All things are possible to them that believe." I saw that wherever Jesus went he looked for faith. He spotted faith.

A woman came through the crowd to Jesus and touched the hem of his garment and she was healed. Jesus turned around and said, "Who touched me?" "Oh," said Peter, "in this crowd of a thousand people anyone could have touched you. What do you mean when you say 'Who touched me?'" "No," said Jesus, "somebody with faith touched me for I felt power go from me." He wasn't satisfied until the poor lady came up and in great embarrassment said, "Lord, I'm the one who touched you." Jesus said, "That's great, sister, that is really great! God bless you! You go in peace. Your faith has made you well." What was it that made her well? Was it Jesus' power, for he said, "I felt power go from me?" Oh yes, that is true, but the thing Jesus was always looking for was faith. When he saw it he signalized it. He blessed it. He encouraged it.

He talked about the seed of faith like the seed of a mustard plant that could move mountains. I tell you that the idea that there is faith that does things was a new one to me and it really set me on a search. "Whatever you ask," said Jesus, "in prayer, believe it. You'll get it." Prayer is the clothes that faith wears. It is believing that gets the answer. Well now, if that is the case, then how do you believe? What are the laws of believing? How do you get that bag of faith that can do things? My heart got hungry to know that. If Moses did his job for God by faith, if Elijah did his job for God by faith, how am I going to do the job God has given me by faith? How do I get the faith to do what God has called me to do? How do I do that?

Then I noticed something which was the second idea that came with great light and help to me. "This is the confidence which we have in him, that if we ask anything according to his will, he hears us and we know that if he hears us, we know we have whatever we have asked of him." We know that he will give the requests that we make of him. The key here is to ask it according to his will. How are you going to know that? So I went back to my own little book, and in my book I saw Mrs. Jones, who asked me to pray for her niece, and I prayed for her. What was I going to ask for her? I don't know. Can I have faith to ask anything for her when I don't know what in the world I am going to ask? I have to tell Mrs Jones, "I'm sorry, Mrs. Jones, I don't know what in the world the will of God is for your niece." I can generally pray, "Dear Lord, bless Mrs. Jones and her niece. Help them to know your will, as I know you want to make that known to them." But beyond that what in the world am I going to ask until I know?

If faith is given according to the will of God, and we know we ask according to his will, then we know that we have the petitions we ask. This puts me right back up against the

business of trying to find out the will of God. I discovered that
seventy per cent of my time was taken up with the consideration of the will of God about matters first, rather than just
praying casually about everything under the sun. If you shoot
at everything in general, you will hit everything in general or
you'll miss everything in general. When you single in and get
clear with God about this or that or the other thing, and know
this is the will of God, that knowledge is faith, for faith comes
by hearing and hearing by the word of God.

This is not just as to our salvation, but also to walking in the
light of his will and fulfilling his purpose. I went back to those
fellows way back in the Old Testament and all through the
Scriptures to see how these men prayed. How did their lives
work in faith? I discovered that their prayers and their faith
were occupied within the scope of their commission from God,
their calling from God. That's what they prayed about. That's
where their faith was exercised and they moved kingdoms.

It was a missionary from Africa that set me on the track of
that. When I began to see some of this whole way of life, I got
desperate for answers. I heard that this missionary, an
Englishman, was coming to New York, so I phoned to New
York and talked to him in his hotel. I asked, "If I come to New
York will you see me?" "Yes," he said, "sure, come on." So I
hitch-hiked to New York and went to the hotel and sat down
with him and brought all my questions to him. Many of the
questions were about praying. I poured them out and said,
"Now what do I do next?"

The blessed missionary looked at me and said, "That's good,
that's really good. You're on the right track. Just keep going."
I said, "Aren't you going to tell me?" "No," he said, "I don't
need to tell you. I don't answer prayers. God does. I can see
you are on the right road. Just keep on going and God will give
you what you need." I left New York and came back to Minneapolis. I felt like a tire that the air had gone out of. I
thought to myself, "That fellow didn't answer even one question. He only said, 'Just keep going; you're on the right track.'"

God works by relationships. He reveals himself. He doesn't
reveal answers. He reveals himself. He is the answer and we
walk, work and live in him. He's our life. He will manifest
himself to us. The Holy Spirit will guide you into all the truth.

He will show you the way and say, "Walk in it, walk in it."

Finally, this leads into more light. He will give you direction, for he works in our hearts both to will and to do his good pleasure. As he gives the direction, he gives faith for it. Faith comes by what God gives. Jesus says, "If you follow me, if you obey me, and my words abide in you and we walk together, you will know me." He reveals himself to people at the point of obedience. And he makes known his will to people at the point of obedience. He fills people with the Holy Spirit at the point of obedience, for, as Peter says in Acts five, he gives the Holy Spirit to them that obey him.

So, we walk by faith, not by sight and not by answers, but by faith in him who leads us, faith in him who is our way.

# 4
# Turmoil

Turmoil! That's the word writers are using to describe our times. It fits the situation almost everywhere.

The vocabulary of the world's troubles is familiar and commonplace: hot and cold war, iron and bamboo curtains, revolution, subversion, racism, riots, strikes, marches, brutality, rebellion. . . .

But this is more than vocabulary. It is realism, a realism that spreads distress and sorrow throughout the world.

Some Christians are so dismayed and disheartened by these conditions that they see little hope for any good except in the return of Jesus Christ to earth in power to subdue the nations. On the outside of the Church whirling storms of evil rip through the nations like tornadoes. On the inside of the Church they see tensions, disputes, heresies, politics and a brash worldliness that threatens the faith with fragmentation, collapse and disaster. What real hope can there be but in Christ's return?

Ultimately this is true. But until the Lord Jesus does return there are a few things we would do well to keep in mind, for if we don't we may miss the challenges, the opportunities and the responsibilities that are given to us in our times. Consider the following, for example:

1—**Turmoil is not something peculiar to our age**. It is not a specialty of our generation. Take up a history book and watch the black chapters of the past go by. Violence filled the earth in Noah's day until God flushed it out by the flood. After a new beginning, it was not long till once again the story of man runs to bloodshed, famine, savagery, slavery, exploitation and wickedness of all kinds.

There was a time when for centuries the Christian churches in Europe prayed fervently for God's protection against the terrible Turks from the south, the Mongols from the east, the Vikings and Barbarians from the north and from the blood purges of the French Revolution in the west. While Christian faith was again and again threatened with defeat and defilement in Europe, the rest of the world sat for long ages in heathen darkness, without hope and without the light and comfort of the gospel of Christ. The turmoil and gloom of past times was every bit as distressing as the worst situation we know in our day and age.

2—**Turmoil in our time seems greater to us and more severe.** The reason is that we are educated to it as previous generations were not. We are informed of all the troubles that exist within moments or hours after their happening. Indeed, we can even see turmoil as it happens on our TV screens. We have a demand, almost a craze, for information and for an analysis of what is happening. Newspeople spare no effort and with courage risk their lives to gather up the news where it happens, even in the hottest spots. The news media then spreads the news out for all to see and hear in word and picture. Never in any former generation has it been done like this.

We are educated to be problem-conscious. This approach to life is given to us from the primary grades and up. Life is a bundle of problems to be studied, analyzed, probed and dealt with. We take this approach into our government, our industry and business, our sciences and human relations. It gives us a front seat view of life as it is in its raw elements, a view of things such as no earlier generation of Christians ever had.

3—**Turmoil is magnified in its dynamics by overcrowding.** Today we are crowded for space. The world has fifteen times more people now than it had in the days of Jesus on earth. In another 150 years there will be fifty billion people on the planet earth. Scientists say that the earth cannot support fifty billion people. With a million more people coming into the human family every seven days, there is bound to be a lot of jostling around to make room for them. The cushioning oceans, deserts and mountain ranges no longer keep us at a distance from each other as they once did.

Today we are also crowded for time by tight schedules, by production deadlines, by swiftly moving transportation, by insistent advertising, by efficiency requirements, by automation and electronics.

In addition our minds are crowded by floods of information, ideas, entertainment, propaganda and knowledge. The public handles all this like it does groceries at the supermarket. It all comes packaged, labeled and priced. People from first-graders to grandmas now talk openly about everything from politics and religion to sex and deodorants like experts. The freedom that comes with this is exhilarating but in many hearts where convictions and faith should rule there is uncertainty and bewilderment.

We are further crowded by monster powers that prowl the earth in search of conquest—money, corporations, big business, towering governments and the grasping ambitions of most organizations. All of this feeds the turmoil of our time and age.

4—**Some of the factors that contribute to turmoil are good.** The Bible and Christian faith have let fly some ideas into the world that are revolutionary and upsetting. The value, worth, dignity and importance of each individual person, whatever may be his lot in life, is one of these explosive ideas. This idea has produced a worldwide concern now for people who before counted for nothing. The very idea of democracy is one fruit of this, as are also the commonly accepted standards for public health, medical services, education and employment. Governments of all the newly independent states of Asia and Africa accept as axiomatic their duty to provide for the well-being of their people. Where formerly it was commonplace for the strong to exploit the weak without shame or protest, there is today a vast awakened insistence on mercy, compassion, brotherhood and respectful equality. This comes from the worldwide scattering of the Word of God.

Science too has opened to the world the hidden secrets of nature and has driven to its dens the dark superstitions that held man captive for so long. Science has found ways to possess, to harness and to distribute t he resources of the earth so as to serve the needs of men. The products of technology now make life more easy, comfortable, safe, interesting and enduring for all of the common people of the world. All of this whipped up by advertising and marketing helps to make the pot boil. People everywhere know now that they can reach the promised land of plenty without having to migrate, and they are impatient with delays.

5—**Some factors that bring on turmoil are decidedly evil.** Past mistakes and wrongs (e.g. slavery and selfish imperialism) that were sown in the wind are now returning in a whirlwind. Demonic powers churn up the temper of rebellion and blind men to Christ the Lord. And the inner "me-first" spirit of unregenerate man, now heightened by the times, is a driving force for turmoil, for it cannot produce anything but turmoil.

Left to itself, our world has no prospect but chaos for there is no way to stop it. The noisy, wacky, lusty violence that now erupts in ugly spasms will be sure to spread corruption everywhere.

6—**God is mindful of the world's turmoil.** The turmoil of the world is not left to itself; God's saving hand is in it. He has not retreated or withdrawn himself but moves in the storm to crowd and press men to his place of mercy. For the turmoil of the world is not something impersonal or merely sociological. Basically it is human, personal. It is a turmoil of people, or rather a turmoil in people.

This is a world of prodigal sons. Some are demanding in shrill voices that the Father give to them a fair and equal share of the inheritance of this world, which for so long has been withheld from them. Others have gotten their share (and much more than their share) of the earth's treasure and are using it up in selfish, riotous living. Still others are washed up, cleaned out, spent and empty-hearted.

Ernest Hemingway said at the end of his tumultuous life that he had lived in a vacuum, as lonely as a radio tube when the batteries are dead and the current is off. And he put a shotgun to his head and pulled the trigger.

Karl Jung, the noted psychiatrist, said that the central neurosis of our times is emptiness—just empty people.

But some of the empty people, like the prodigal son, are thinking wistfully of the Father's house and are coming home to the Father who waits for them. And some of them, after the restoration feast is over, are going manfully out into the turmoil of the world in the power of the Holy Spirit, no longer to be overcome by evil but "to overcome evil with good."

It is quite possible to be so distracted by the turmoil, tumult and confusion of our times that we do not perceive God's mighty hand mercifully outstretched in the world to save. And it is also possible to be so concerned about saving ourselves and what is ours from the storms that blow that we miss our mission from God to the world.

# 5

# The World Crucified

*Part of a transcribed message given on the evening of August 7, 1972, at Camp Wanamingo.*

In John 13 Jesus acted out, as it were, a parable by washing the disciples' feet. This parable spoke of his mission in the world which culminated in a cross. In many ways that foot-washing is a symbol and a parable of the whole way of the cross in the life of Jesus.

Now I'd like to take up that thought as seen in the words of Saint Paul in writing to the Galatians (read Gal. 6:11-18).

Let us pray: We turn gratefully again to your Word, O God our Father. We thank you that we see Jesus here. We thank you that we see in these pages what he has done to save us from our sins and to make it possible for us to be friends and the children of God. We pray that we may once again be drawn to love Jesus, trust him, follow him, and count him our treasure, our joy and our all in all. Amen.

In verse fourteen of Galatians six Paul says, "But far be it from me to glory, (or to boast), except in the cross of our Lord Jesus Christ through which, (or by which), this world has been crucified to me and I have been crucified to this world." We live a large part of our lives by the use of symbols. We have symbolism in nearly every aspect of our living. By symbols we express some of the things we hold dear; some of the things we believe most firmly; some of the goals we pursue most persistently. These are expressed in symbols. This is true of religion, or government, or education, or of the common relationships we have with each other in daily life.

Have you been in a Greek Orthodox church and seen some of the symbols such as the icons or perhaps a large picture of Saint George on a huge horse with a big, long spear that he used to thrust into the devil? Those are symbols that speak very strongly to the heart and faith of the people in the Greek Orthodox Church.

In large parts of Asia are followers of the Buddha. In Southeast Asia, China, Burma, Tibet and other such places you will find the symbol of the lotus flower which Buddhism has taken over as a symbol of its faith. It is one of the loveliest of flowers with its bowl-like pink and white petals. There are pictures and statues of Buddha sitting cross-legged in the middle of the lotus with his hands resting gently in his lap. This is to them a symbol of serenity, peace and rest, a symbol of deliverance from the stresses, torments and twistedness of life.

For Muslims Mecca is the symbol of their faith. Five times a day they turn toward the city of Mecca in prayer. One night in western Pakistan, I shared a railway compartment with a Pakistani lawyer and his son. Both of them spoke excellent English; mine was shabby alongside of theirs. We sat and talked into the late afternoon and evening. As we settled down for the night, I wondered if being devout Muslims they would pray and, if so, how on earth they were going to tell on this train in what direction Mecca was. After they had used a pitcher of water to wash their arms, ears and mouth, the father took out a compass and after studying it, adjusted his prayer rug and faced toward Mecca. For him and four hundred million people like him, Mecca is the symbol in their faith for all that Allah (God) does for them.

I saw in China, before the communists took over the country, slashed in black characters on the sides of buildings here and there some of the slogans of the Chinese Communist Revolution. Once in a while you could hear these slogans sung or shouted by the crowds. One such symbol of their revolution was, "There is no god; there is no devil; do not be afraid."

There are other kinds of symbols. Our national flag is a symbol. It is a symbol of the Constitution. It is a symbol of the history of our people. It is a symbol of the aims, hopes, aspirations and treasure of our nation. So also a ring is a symbol. When people get married, I don't suppose there are many who do so without the use of a ring. This simple symbol says much about the family, its hopes, its loyalties, its blessings. It's a symbol.

Now the same is true for Paul. He too had a symbol and he had a slogan. It is found in the verse I quoted, "Far be it from me to boast in anything except in the cross of our Lord Jesus Christ, for through this cross I have been crucified to this world and this world has been crucified to me." The cross of Christ has severed me forever from this world and it has separated this world from me.

Now, of course, Paul was not talking about the wooden cross itself. So also, when he says he is crucified to this world, he does not mean this world of nature nor does he mean this world of people. What then does he mean by the cross? He means whatever happened to Jesus as he was pounded to the cross, put to death, buried and raised again. It's what took place in the whole unfolding of the life and mission of Jesus in this world and its culmination on the cross and the victory in the resurrection and the ascension into heaven. He glories in all of that which is symbolized in the cross. By that cross Paul discovered that he was set free from "this world." If the world was not the world of nature, mountains, rivers, lakes, butterflies, etc., nor the world of people, what world was it then? It was the world of ideas, ambitions, dispositions, outlook, mind and temper by which this world lives apart from God. That's what is meant by "this world".

Now I'd like to examine this a little more closely with you. What ideas, what values, what goals and what motives of this world have been crucified with Christ? There are many of them, but here are five which to me are very meaningful and significant.

**1—One idea in this world is that salvation, or the favor of God, comes to those who work for it,** who have earned it and make themselves worthy of it.

This is what the New Testament calls self-righteousness, making yourself acceptable and right with God by whatever you think or do. This idea is wide-spread throughout the world. It is common everywhere. It is age old. And it makes common sense in a worldly way. But this idea has been crucified by the cross of Jesus.

At times we ask people the question: "If you were now to come to heaven's gate and wanted to get in, on what grounds would you expect God to take you in?" Some people say, "Well, I'm as good as the next fellow. I really haven't done anything too bad. I'm tending to business and as far as I know I certainly think God would want me in heaven." Well, that is the idea, says the New Testament, which has been crucified on the cross of Jesus—that worldly idea.

Paul saw that in the cross of Jesus, God gave his favor, not to the deserving, but to the undeserving. There on that very cross the whole worldly idea that men make themselves worthy of the paradise was put death. It was killed for St. Paul. "If anybody," he says, "deserves to go to heaven or be right with God, it is I. I came from the tribe of Benjamin. I was raised a Pharisee. I never knew a single thing against me all those years I was serving God. But I do not boast in anything." Nothing! Not even in his conversion. Who can point to a conversion like that of the Apostle Paul? Much as Paul enjoyed looking back at it and talking about it, praising God for it, it was not grounds for his boasting. He never boasted in that but only in the cross. He said, "I have found that on the cross God came and took my sins away. I'm justified by faith in the cross of Christ." This Paul calls "my gospel." This was the good news he was preaching about Jesus and it was in that that he boasted.

Where can I find my hope of God's favor? It does not lie in my background. It does not lie in my race. It does not lie in my experiences. It does not lie in my forefathers. It does not lie in my belonging to a particular church. It does not lie in the knowledge I have gleaned over the years. It lies only in the cross of Jesus where he took me and my sins into himself and carried my wickedness away and gave to me by his blood the forgiveness of sin from God my Father. In that I hope. I learned that from Saint Paul, for his hope was in the cross of Jesus and no place else. That's where God put to death the worldly idea that somehow we shall find favor with him by meriting it, earning it, or being worthy of it.

2—There is another worldly idea that is very common. That is the world's idea of what really constitutes a good life.

We have a whole lot of this idea in America. Just take a look at the *Good Housekeeping* magazine and turn its pages and look at what they think the good life is. Or get the great, big, thick book from Sears and look through it. Here you see a whole world of wonderful things. "This is the good life," they say. "Have it all!" And they say more than that; every page is saying to you, "Friend, you need, you deserve it. This is yours. Come and get it. If you can't pay for it now, get it anyway and pay for it later. That's how much you deserve it. Don't go without it."

What kind of a life is it that everybody wants, that everybody is chasing after and seeking? "Well," says the world, "the fullness of life, or the good life, consists in the abundance of what a person can accumulate." Get all you can of everything you can, is the world's way to the good life.

But when you come to the cross and look at Jesus hanging there, you see a man who spoke to this world about the good life and said: "I came to give men life and to give it to them abundantly." Yet there he hung between heaven and earth, stripped naked with flies buzzing around his wounds. They spat on him! They despised him, he was hated, rejected and scorned! This man speaks about the abundant life?

Now there is a big difference between the kind of abundance that Jesus talks about and the kind there is apart from the cross. The cross has put to death the world's idea of what the abundant life is. The abundant life apparently does not consist in what a man possesses, since he who had the fullness of life died with nothing to his name and was buried in a borrowed tomb. He said to people, "You want to follow me? Let me tell you, the foxes have holes and the birds of the air have nests, but I don't have any place to lay my head. Do you want to follow me?"

In the second place, the world says the good life consists of self realization. Get ahead! Succeed! Dream big! Shoot high! Become all that you are wanting to be! Why allow yourself to be stuck in the mud? There is opportunity; get out and make something of it. Have you ever heard sentiments like that?

But here is Jesus who had the fulness of life and about whom the Scriptures say, "Though he was in the form of God, he emptied himself and took the form of a servant and being made in the likeness of men, he humbled himself." Here obviously was a man who was not trying somehow for self-realization. He was living for something else, as he said all through his life: "I come not to do my own will; I seek only to do the will of him who sent me." When he came to the end of his earthly life, he turned to his father and said, "Father, I have done what you sent me to do. It is all done. I am coming home to you." There is the fullness of life! The cross holds that out as fullness of life, not self-realization.

Yet another worldly idea that was crucified is that the good life consists in peace of mind. Get free from anxiety and cares. Be jolly, relax, be at ease.

When I turn to look at Jesus, I see a man who was troubled in soul. "He was a man of sorrows," says Isaiah, "and acquainted with grief." He was troubled; he was a man of grief. Whose grief? He carried the world's grief; he bore our sins on the cross. Yet he had peace of mind—not the world's peace of mind, but he had God's peace of mind that nobody could take from him. That peace made it possible for him to carry the burdens of this world, not to avoid them.

Still another worldly idea that was put to death at the cross was the world's idea that the good life consists of popularity. The people of the world want to be accepted, to be admitted, to be respected and to be wanted. The followers of Jesus are not going around in the world looking for popularity because they live at the cross. For them the abundant life does not consist of what the world thinks of them; the abundant life is the life in the Lord Jesus.

Let us add a further item. At the cross the worldly idea that the good life consists of security was put permanently to death. The world seeks security against all kinds of failures and disasters. It is terrible for calamities to come. When that happens the good life goes out the window, as when your house is struck by lightning or blown down in a storm. There goes the good life out the window when your business fails, or you have a nervous breakdown or are laid up in a hospital. There goes the good life out the window when all the good things you have tried to do come to nothing.

But there I see hanging on a cross a good man, the best man that ever walked on this earth, God's beloved Son, spotless, pure, undefiled, though he was attacked by every foe and temptation that has come to man. There he hangs. It looks like his life had become a terrible failure, yet he talked about the abundant life. He turned his back on all worldly security, or the use of his supernatural power to defend himself as well as the defense his friends would have given him. He said no to it all because the good life did not consist of bolstering his life with all kinds of worldly security against failure. That idea was put to death on the cross. In its place God gives us another kind of security. It is a security where he keeps us "by his power unto a salvation to be revealed at the last time."

Finally, there is the worldly idea that the good life is the life that survives for many long years to a ripe old age. It is like getting to be ninety years of age and still able to walk around and to look back and recall that you were happy all along the way, every day, every blessed day.

Here I see Jesus who came from heaven with fullness of life, but at the age of barely thirty, he is hung upon a cross, to die. He had run his course in a third of a century, only half the life-time of most people. But he had fulfilled his ministry. He had done all that God gave him to do. His hour had come. And so he gave up his spirit.

So, that is the Jesus who came to give men abundant life. The cross separated him and his kind of abundant life from the worldly idea of the good life. On the other side of the cross the resurrection introduces all men to another kind of full-ness of life—the life in Jesus.

3—**The world's idea that sin and wrong are not too serious** was also killed at the cross.

Things that are called sin and wrong the world nowadays says are relative matters. Everybody does them and they change with the times. They are sort of part of our culture and are largely determined by environment or by heredity. God understands this and will not hold it against us; don't panic, it will all come out in the wash, so to say.

But the cross of Jesus makes a clean break with this kind

of thinking. The Son of God was made sin on our behalf and came under the wrath and judgment of God. Because of our sins, "He was smitten by God and afflicted . . . and the Lord has laid on him the iniquity of us all", says Isaiah. If the cross says anything at all it says that sin is serious. God does not tolerate it. God will judge it. He judged it in his Son on the cross. Therefore, for those who come to him and trust in him the judgment will pass. Only then will we hear God's word of forgiveness.

**4—In the fourth place, a worldly idea that was put to death on the cross is the idea that love is an aesthetic response to what is lovely and beautiful.**
We commonly hear of this kind of love. For instance when a song is sung someone will exclaim, "Oh, I just love it!" Or somebody puts together a tasty recipe for pork chops and potatoes and a big husky guy sits up to the table and says, "Yum-m-m, I just love this." Or a young man sees a lady walk by and he tells himself, "Wow! I could sure go for her! I could really love that girl." All that kind of love does not appear at the cross. Here another kind of love is displayed, God's love, Calvary love, which is God's response to ugly, dirty, wicked, unlovely and cursed people. "In this is love," says Saint John, "not that we loved God, but that he loved us and gave his Son to be the expiation for our sins," the only way by which our sins can be forgiven.

**5—Then fifth, there is another worldly idea that was put to death at the cross and that is the idea that our assets make us masters and creditors** rather than servants and debtors to others.
That which we are by race, what we own either by inheritance or by our own efforts, what we have by way of position in society, what we have of abilities and good fortune—all this puts us in a gainful position. But at the cross you see Jesus, he who made and sustains all things, he who owns everything and to whom all things belong, giving his life for sinners. Paul in looking to Jesus saw from the cross that the blessings we have make us debtors both to God and our fellow men. This is an indebtedness that comes from love. It is strange and

hard to understand. Love feels best when it owes the best it possesses to others, and gives it away.

Now in closing let us note what this boasting in the cross did for the Apostle Paul. Notice seven things suggested in Galations six:

1. He was delivered from being self-centered to live a life that was centered in Christ.

2. He entered into a fellowship with Jesus' sufferings that brought him close to the life, mission and purpose of Jesus.

3. He entered into a way of life that left the marks of the cross on his body.

4. He found a whole new dimension of life, beyond the law, ritual and formalism in the new creation of the resurrection life of Jesus.

5. He became a servant to other people, and like Jesus he lived not to be ministered to but to minister to others.

6. He received a benediction: "peace and mercy". If you desire to be blessed with God's peace and God's mercy all the days of your life, then walk as Paul did, with the cross.

7. He found himself in good company. The way of the cross put him in the fellowship, the family, the household of God, into the Israel of God, God's own people.

I have just been relating to you what Paul discovered in the cross and we have heard Paul tell of his boasting in the cross. Does it evoke a response in our hearts to want to join him and glory in the cross with him?

# 6

# Objectives in Mission

*From a 1972 Fellowship Week message, Lutheran Bible Institute. Camrose, Alberta, Canada.*

I'd like to think with you about the common task we all have from our Lord Jesus Christ of taking the good news of his salvation to all the world. We can see how this was carried out in the Early Church and how it has been carried out these two thousand years by earnest Christian people in their generations. However, anyone reading the story will see that this task is not an easy one, nor has it been taken for granted by the Church as a whole that this is its task. Sometimes there have been whole generations, indeed centuries, that have gone by when this task seems to have been lost sight of. Today we are living in an unusual time as far as church history goes. There hasn't been a time since the earliest days of Christianity when so many Christian people have had a part in carrying out this commission of our Lord.

In our Lutheran Church, for example, in these past four hundred and fifty years or so, this task has not been generally accepted, or understood, or followed. It has been an uphill effort all through these many centuries to take seriously the call of God, generation by generation, and to bend our efforts and our strength and as his people to give priority to the matter of taking to people everywhere the good news of how they may be saved by faith in Jesus Christ.

Now in our day this has become a very great, wonderful and widespread movement—a mission movement. From North America, I suppose, we have about forty thousand Protestant missionaries. There are as many Roman Catholic missionaries and maybe more. These forty thousand missionaries scattered across the world, in a hundred different countries, every day use more than a thousand languages to tell the good news of Jesus. That is a very heartening thing to see.

Now my question is: What are they doing? What does the missionary movement aim to do? What's our job? Now I'd like to suggest that there are four basic aims. Somehow in the whole process of the missionary movement throughout the world there are four functions, four ministries, four aims:

1. To evangelize.
2. To make disciples.
3. To form churches.
4. To do good.

Now let's have a look at each of them.

1—**To Evangelize.** The Bible Society has a very appealing drawing that epitomizes its goal. It pictures a farmer with a bag of seed over his shoulder. As he walks along he reaches into the bag, takes a handful of seed—whether it is corn, wheat or whatever— and scatters it all over the ground. That is the idea of evangelizing. The seed is the Word of God. The major object of mission is to scatter the seed of God's Word into every part of the world. By the scattering of the Word of God to enlighten this dark world, men receive the gift of repentance and faith and come to salvation.

My father was a missionary in China, and so I grew up with this idea. He regarded his daily job to be to scatter the Word of God. I was the oldest of three brothers and as we grew up our father had us go along with him, each with a bag of tracts, and pass out Christian literature to people we met along the road. We would say, "Take this and read it. It will lead you to know God." In this way we had a share in scattering the seed of God's Word in the world.

To do that job requires three things. Obviously it takes mobility. That is why Jesus said, "Go into all the world and preach the gospel." His disciples could not sit in Jerusalem and evangelize the world. A farmer cannot sit on his back porch and scatter the seed over his field. It requires mobility. You see this in Jesus and the Apostle Paul. You see it in the whole missionary movement. The Christian mission involves going to the farthest reaches of the earth to scatter the Word of God.

The second thing about evangelism is, the Word of God should reach everybody so that nobody is missed. "God would have all men to be saved and come to the knowledge of the truth," wrote the Apostle Paul. The calling our Lord has given us to evangelize the world means to cover every person who can possibly be reached, friend and foe alike.

The third thing about scattering the seed is that it should be preached. There is a sense of urgency about it. There is the pressure of time, whether you think of it in the long-range term of history or simply in terms of our generation, or within the limits of your own lifetime, or your own strength.

As we seek to scatter the seed of God's Word, we of course will meet up with all kinds of problems. Language problems, expenses, government restrictions, competing ideas and religions, resentment by people opposed to the gospel, travel problems and the opposition of Satan.

2—**To Make Disciples.** In some ways, of course, this follows naturally on evangelizing. The purpose of preaching is to lead people to become followers and disciples of Jesus.

There are three things involved in making disciples. First is persuasion. It is interesting to see how Luke, who describes the missionary journeys of St. Paul, takes note of how persuasive Paul was. He pleads and beseeches men to believe that Jesus is the Messiah, the Sent One from God and that there is no hope apart from him.

Second is baptism. Jesus said, "Make disciples of all nations, baptizing them in the name of the Father and of the Son and of the Holy Spirit." The New Testament has a very sharp outlook upon baptism; it makes it a very decisive matter. To bring a person to baptism is a very strong step in making a disciple. It is a public act by which one breaks with the world and comes into union with Christ.

There are, however, problems that come with baptism. In the whole business of missions around the world, this matter of baptizing comes into some very rocky and troublesome times. There are questions of qualification. There is also the question, should people be baptized one by one, or by whole families, or by entire tribes? There is also the question of when baptism is valid. So there are problems in this matter of baptism that have not been ironed out.

Third is obedience. Jesus said, "Teach them to obey all that I have commanded you." Salvation, if it is to be true salvation, is to restore obedience to God. The break with God came at the point of disobedience. "By the disobedience of one, the many were made sinners," wrote St. Paul. The whole point of Jesus' coming into the world is that men and women who walked away in disobedience might now be restored to a life of obedience to God. How do you teach people to obey all that Jesus has commanded? Well, by what the Scriptures say, by example, and by the agreement of the fellowship of God's people. There is that constant, adjusting discipline wherever you have a live fellowship of God's people.

3—**To Form Churches.** The New Testament never speaks of Christian faith and life apart from the church. We're not on private pilgrimages. We're born into the family of God. The ministry of Jesus, the letters of the New Testament and all that is said about the life of God is dealt with in terms of the corporate body of God's people—his family, his household, his church. Wherever you find Christian people they cluster together. "Wherever two or three of you are gathered together in my name," said Jesus, "There I am in your midst— in your company."

In the forming of churches, Christians have tried somehow to express their understanding of the nature of the church. Historically, I suppose one of the plainest expressions of this is in the Nicene Creed, which dates back to 325 A.D. Those who attended that council meeting said about the church, that they believed it to be one, holy, catholic, and apostolic. These are the four basic characteristics of the Church.

It is one Church. The unity of the Church is a gift from God. It is not something that we organize and bring about ourselves. But we are to maintain that unity, and as far as we can, live by it, walk in it, submit to it and find joy in it together. So in forming churches around the world, it has been a concern of missionaries that the Church might be one.

It is a holy Church. It is holy, not by its own achievements or by its own perfections, but it is holy because of the word of forgiveness spoken to us from the cross. A holy church is a church that is wholly his. It belongs to him. The big question is, how do you keep it that way? This is something Christians have wrestled with all through the centuries, and even now are constantly working at.

It is a catholic Church. That means that it is for all people, all races of people, all castes of people, all kinds of people. It also means that in any place in the world, where the Christian faith takes root, the Church becomes native there. It is not an American or Canadian or European church; it is a catholic church. It can become a Christian church on any soil in any place. In that sense catholic means universal.

It is an apostolic Church. That means that in its teachings, its fellowship and its programs, the church goes back to the apostles through whom the gospel was given to us, and we look there for our foundations and for our norms. Some people have problems with this. They differ about this and thus we have all these different kinds of denominations. Christians will agree as to the simple, basic truths of the gospel. We will agree that God loves this world and has given his Son to die for it and that by faith in Jesus we may be recovered, restored and reconciled to God. But on the basic question as to how the grace of God is ministered to people there is a difference of views. There is a lot of overlapping but four rather distinctive differences. With some is the idea that the grace of God comes through the priesthood. Then there are those who say the grace of God comes through his Word and his sacraments. Another branch of Christians emphasize that God's grace comes through the response of faith. Yet another idea is that the grace of God comes by personal encounter, in some mystical experience, without the help of priests, God's Word, the sacraments or the church.

4—**To Do Good.** It was said about our Lord Jesus, "He went about doing good." The apostles urged, "Do not be overcome by evil, but overcome evil with good." Missionaries in the last couple of hundred years especially have gone out to other lands with three concerns when it comes to doing good.

The early missionary societies had a concern to "civilize." This went hand in hand with preaching the gospel. They felt that they should carry with them the best that God had given them to help other people to meet their needs. These people took with them their trades, their skills and their abilities in the name of Jesus together with the gospel. They sought to bring all those things that they believed were of value and were necessary for improvement of life to share with people to whom they came bringing the message of Jesus. All of life was seen to be a life that was lived under God. It should all be developed for God's glory and to serve God. That was their idea of civilization. So when they went abroad to preach the gospel, they carried this idea with them, trying to bring all of life everywhere under the rule of Christ and his kingdom.

In the second place, they had a concern for human need. Wherever the missionaries went there was poverty, sickness, ignorance, hunger, filth, suffering and misfortune. They read in their Bibles that they were to bear one another's burdens. And so there has gone along with the missionary movement an effort to meet the human needs of people.

In the third place, there has been a concern to right things that are wrong. In this perverted world there is injustice, slavery, violation of human rights, terrible treatment of prisoners, oppression of the poor, the bondage of caste, opium addiction, foot binding in China and widow burning in India. Missionaries have felt that it is part of their calling to try to correct the wrongs and champion efforts for right in society.

To overcome evil with good takes direct contact with trouble, and requires godly men and women to be living as "shining lights" in dark places. To overcome evil with good requires strong, Christian congregations in the midst of a "crooked and perverse generation." To overcome evil with good calls for the constant service of ministering love by men and women who together live under the grace and rule of God and his Word. So Paul says, "We preach Christ Jesus as Lord and ourselves as your servants for Jesus' sake." Proclamation and service go hand in hand.

And so the missionary movement across the world today continues to move on, true to its calling, aiming in the four directions of evangelism, discipling, church building and doing good.

# 7
# Our Ministry

*Part of a transcribed message; one in a series of Bible studies on Second Corinthians presented in June 1971.*

In our Bible studies we turn to Second Corinthians in which the Apostle Paul discusses what he calls our ministry. He, of course, draws upon his own experience as a missionary, teacher, preacher and pastor in speaking about that ministry. But it is not his own private ministry that he is talking about. He speaks of it as the common calling, work, service and ministry of all God's people in his church. He speaks of it as our ministry.

Let us note first the setting for Paul's ministry—Corinth. It was a city located on the isthmus which joins the north and south of Greece; this was strategic since trade routes from north and south as well as east and west crossed here. Therefore, it was a good market; therefore, it had a mixture of peoples; therefore, it was a strong government center under Rome. And at the same time it was a wicked city with a temple erected to the erotic goddess of love. Paul came to this city (Acts 18), won the chief of the synagogue and a few others to the Christian faith, and these believers formed the church in Corinth to whom Paul later writes this letter.

In Second Corinthians, chapters two and three, Paul points out the glories of our ministry. First, *the character of the ministry*—as believers in Christ we are part of his victory procession and we spread the aroma of Christ and we are commissioned of God to testify to Christ. Second, *the creden-*

*tials of our ministry*—those who were converted through
Paul's ministry were open letters of recommendation, written
by the Spirit of God. Third, *the substance of our ministry*—
in contrast to the written code given through Moses, the new
covenant in Christ is marked by life and hope and freedom.
Fourth, *confidence of our ministry*—since this ministry
comes from God himself, we are bold in presenting it to men.

Paul, in chapters three and four, also notes *the problems in
the ministry*. For all of its joy and glory, the ministry also has
its difficulties and problems. Out of all the problems, he
singles out two that were particularly vexing to him. The first
was the veil that lies over the hearts and minds of people
when confronted with the gospel. The second was a personal
bodily difficulty which seemingly he had all the time.

In Second Corinthians, chapter five, Paul deals with *the
motives in our ministry*. After warning about false motives,
he speaks of persuading men out of the fear of the Lord. But
the basic motivation is the love of Christ which constrains
him.

Continuing on in the same chapter Paul deals with *the
message of our ministry*. It is basically a message of reconciliation between God and man through Jesus Christ. We are
called to be ambassadors of this message to all men.

In chapters six through nine of Second Corinthians, we
come to a discussion of *the responsibilities of our ministry*.
Says Paul, "As servants of God we commend ourselves in
every way." In all he lists twenty-eight different situations.
First, he links nine of them in one category of three parts each;
next, he lumps nine more in another large category with three
sections in each; and then, he puts the rest together in a
wonderful, lyrical passage of contrasts.

In the first section, the responsibilities are personal. There
is a negative aspect to it, "We put no obstacle in any one's way,
so that no fault may be found with our ministry." On the
positive side it is to commend ourselves to every man's
conscience in the sight of God. We are not really effective until
somehow by our message we reach a man's conscience—not
simply his mind, not just his thinking, but his conscience in
which he is related morally to God. He is answerable to God.
He has to stand up not merely with some thoughts about God,

but he stands in a position of responsibility to God.

In the second section, from 6:11 to chapter 9, Paul deals with the responsibility of our ministry to the church or congregation. He deals here with only two responsibilities: to work for harmony in the congregation, and to work for generosity in the life of the congregation.

In 6:14 to 7:16 Paul addresses the matter of working for the unity of the church. That is something that was badly needed in Corinth. Disunity in the congregation was one of their major problems. They were split off into all kinds of factions as told in 1 Corinthians 1:10-13. There got to be some bad feelings amongst them and this just divided the strength of the congregation.

Now then, since that is the problem, how do you work for harmony. Paul has three things to say about it. One, he says, "Be large hearted!" He mentions four things about being large hearted: "Open your mouth to one another." If we are going to have harmony in a congregation, it means we must be open mouthed with other people. Talk to them, talk freely, share with them, find out who they are and get into a good conversation. Next Paul says we are to open our affections to one another. If you are going to work for harmony, then don't hold back your affections from other people in the congregation. Then third, he says, "Be careful for each other." Have care and consideration for each other. We are to care about our fellow Christians in the congregation when they have this or that problem or difficulty. Have a care for each other if there is to be a large heartedness. The fourth thing Paul suggests is that we ought to comfort one another. Paul has been working hard on all their troubles and failures, yet look how he talks to them. All right, I have great confidence in you. I have great pride in you. I am filled with comfort. I am overjoyed in you. To be largehearted, let us express genuine confidence and trust toward each other.

The second thing Paul suggests in order to keep harmony in the congregation is for the Christians to draw the line on some things. In the section 6:14-18 he discusses how the congregation will need again and again to draw some distinct lines that preserve the character of the congregation in its integrity, its place of work, its ministry and its life before God. He says two things: "Do not be mismated with unbelievers;" and "Come out from among them and be separated from them."

Now, may I make a few comments about this. There are some things that just do not go with Christian faith and life. They are not only unseemly, they are incompatible. This is the whole idea of being mismated with unbelievers. We are people who belong to God and live under God in his kingdom and serve him. And so we are different from this world, which does not follow God, is not given to God, and is not seeking to do his will.

There needs to be a place at which God's people draw the line and come out from the world around them and are separated. However, no man is a keeper of another man's conscience on these things. Each one will have to draw the line in his own life on personal matters. But here in this situation Paul is suggesting that the congregation needs to draw a line on such matters. The church is in constant danger of being sucked into the course of this world. So over the years the church has learned to draw its line.

In chapter 7:15-16 Paul brings out the third thing needed to achieve unity in the church. There are times when the church needs to be rebuked. Paul spoke his rebuke to the church in Corinth when the church was in a real mess. Paul spoke his words of rebuke from a position of authority and responsibility as an apostle and as the founder of the church. Paul spoke his rebuke hesitantly, reluctantly and in inner anguish. But when things had gone so far, and become too intolerable, there was nothing else to do but to rebuke the church for the wrong. Paul's rebuke was spoken in phases. He did it by letter; he did it by personal visit; then he sent Titus as his personal agent. What is important to note is that his rebuke was not to condemn the church, but to help the church to repentance and to recover its right relationship to God. He kept pushing it through until he could help the church to come to a real, free repentance toward God. Finally, notice that Paul in rebuking was at the same time quick with his words of praise as soon as he saw that his rebuke had taken effect. He is quick to pick up every positive thing he can see in the church to strengthen it. This then covers the matter of how to work for harmony in the church.

In chapters eight and nine, Paul deals with another matter —how to work for generosity in the congregation. It related to a particular situation. An awful famine had come along so that the church in Jerusalem was really up against it and in tough shape, very poor and suffering.

Paul got burdened about the church in Jerusalem, even though they didn't like him too well. He started a project and so began to pass the word around among all the congregations that had been begotten by the mother church in Jerusalem. He said, "How about taking up some offerings now in the churches? We will send the money to the church in Jerusalem to help them now in this time of famine and hardship." That's what he talked about when he wrote to the church in Corinth. He is getting them to take up a good collection there to send to the old mother church in Jerusalem.

As he handles this particular problem in these two chapters, Paul teaches some principles and methods of dealing with money in the church. But as our time is gone, you will have to work out the details on your own.

# 8

# Personal Piety and Social Awareness

*A personal letter to a former staff member, dated April 28, 1969.*

Dear _____,

There is no easy answer to your question as to why it is that so often those who emphasize social awareness in churches forget the personal devotional part of Christianity, and those who are strong on the latter often ignore social responsibility. Now and then *Christianity Today* carries articles on this question, and there is quite a bit of discussion in evangelical circles about this.

May I say just two things that come to me on this issue? First, I think that the accusation that pietistic Christians have not been concerned with the social needs and physical needs of people is magnified in most instances far beyond the truth.

The great humanitarian and human rights movements of the past century or more are rooted not in liberal, humanist churches but in revival movements in conservative churches. This was true of the Wesleyan revival of England when, along with preaching repentance and the new birth, there was also a strong concern over the filth in the cities, bad housing for the poor, child labor, no curb on liquor, and the unrighteous slave traffic. It stirred all England to the very bottom and without

a doubt saved England from the kind of blood bath that came
to France in 1848.

The great missionaries who sought the personal salvation
and conversion of people through preaching and repentance
were the leaders in all the movements that raced across the
world to stamp out slavery, to champion the needs of the
outcast, to work for prison reforms, to fight epidemics, to heal
the sick, to enlighten the minds of men with knowledge and
education, to sow the seeds that would fire the souls of men
with longings for liberty, equality and fraternity.

It was out of the Evangelical Revival in this country, out of
the stirring of the Spirit from the preaching of men like
Finney, Whitfield, Moody and others like them that there
came the society-building movements of the Salvation Army
and the Young Men's Christian Association. Dr. John R. Mott
was not only the gifted leader of the Student Volunteer
Movement, but he personally went and spread the YMCA in
80 nations of the world to lift and cleanse, help and enrich
people in their daily life.

I have been firmly convinced that the springs of social
concern are not to be found in the humanist churches so much
as in the pietist churches of the past two centuries. And I
think that while it has been very hard to press upon people the
claims of God for personal dealings with him, it has been
much easier to press upon people the claims of God for the
earthly good of mankind. The latter has been so successful,
in fact, that governments by and large have become socialist
and regard as axiomatic their responsibility to care for their
people and to work for their protection, welfare and dignity.
And there has developed widely a very sensitive and determined social conscience toward the rights of men. The
preaching that in the long run produced this kind of fruit was
a John the Baptist type of preaching—judgment, repentance
toward God and remaking of daily life to conform to the will
of God for mankind. But the vertical dimension of this kind
of preaching has been largely ignored, while the horizontal
dimension of the preaching has caught on like a prairie fire
everywhere. My point is that this fire did not come from the
humanists but from the pietists.

Second, while I believe this to be true, I must say that the social side of the church's concern runs competition with other equally strong concerns and has at times been smothered by them. There are at least three other concerns that have taken the attention of the conservative churches.

**1—The Concern for Purity.** It was a twofold concern: purity of doctrine and teaching, and purity of personal life before God. Both of these are constantly being threatened by the world and it has been only natural that Christians have been suspicious of the world, have seen the world to be their foe, and have tended to avoid too close involvement with the world. It is also easy to see why when humanists, who do as they please with the Bible, go all out for human rights, pious believers tend to keep back from joining them in social action.

**2—The Concern for Unity.** This is not only a sound, biblical doctrine but it is a very strong imperative of the Holy Spirit in the life of believers. While the unity of the Spirit in the life of the Church is the gift of God and is not something that can be achieved by the arts of men, yet this God-given unity must be nurtured, preserved and cultivated. There has been need for this because many things work powerfully to break the Church into fragments. And therefore, it is easy to see that Christianity has been right in concerning itself with unity in the house of faith. All churches have been doing this in the USA. Lutherans once were a scattering of more than a hundred different, feeble synods. But within a century these bits have been coming together more and more until now they are close to becoming a single family of churches.

**3—The Concern for Mission.** It is a concern for sound and faithful preaching of God's Word that will bring people to repentance toward God and faith toward Jesus Christ. The humanists have been shouting up and down the land that God is Father of all and we are all brothers of Jesus and that therefore we should make our land a happy homeland for all of God's children. The pietist-minded believers and church leaders have stayed clear of this because to them this is a perishing world, under the wrath of God, and to them all men are lost until they are born of the Holy Spirit and washed clean in the shed blood of Christ, and are thus redeemed and reconciled to God.

Among Lutherans for the past one hundred years in this land these concerns have been foremost: to keep purity, to hold unity, and to work for the regeneration of the unsaved. The Lutheran churches adopted strong confessional creeds, carried out thorough training programs in Sunday schools, confirmation classes, parochial schools, and carefully guarded theological seminaries. Also, since most Lutherans were immigrants from Europe, the first concern was to reach all those who came from Europe and try to save them and to hold them for God in his Church. They generally used the languages of the old countries until just forty years ago. They had their hands so full doing all these things that they just didn't have time to think of the Indians, Irish, Negroes, Greeks and all the rest. As newcomers themselves, they had their hands full with homesteading, raising big families, building houses, farms, shops, schools, churches and colleges. As most of them were farmers, they were far removed from the city slums, ghettos and Mafia.

Today the pattern of life is greatly changed. In our Lutheran churches there is coming to be a wide concern for social problems. But with this there appears to be a decided relaxation of interest in purity of life, spiritual unity and conversion of the unsaved.

How can all of these concerns be kept vital and in balance? That is a question to really tussle with.

In Christian Fellowship,
*Paul J. Lindell*

# 9

# The Story of
# WMPL Beginnings

*Part of a transcribed message by Paul given in April 1972
at St. Peter's Lutheran Church, Norwalk, Ohio.*

In the tenth chapter of the Gospel of John Jesus calls
himself the Good Shepherd, he says that believing people are
the sheep, the flock that he cares for. Having talked about the
flock, having talked about the sheep, in verse sixteen he goes
on to say that he looks beyond the flock, he looks beyond the
sheep and says, "There are other sheep who are not of this
fold. Them also I must bring and they shall be one flock with
us and one shepherd." Now obviously he is talking about the
whole great world of people who live away from God. Those
who go on day after day looking after their daily life without
being subject to God, without knowing him, having no hope,
as St. Paul says, and without God in this world. Those are the
other sheep that he wants to bring into the flock.

Now, how does he do that? How does our Shepherd reach
out for those other sheep? How does he go about getting
them? How does he find them? How does he go about calling
them? How does he add them to his flock? Let me give you
an illustration of how he does it:

In the second and third chapter of Exodus we read about a
shepherd who lived, O maybe, almost 3,500 years ago. I
picture him with a long tough beard and long hair and a long
eastern garment. I picture him wandering around the sand
hills with a long shepherd staff in his hand and a large flock
of maybe three or four hundred sheep. He is herding these

sheep in a very unfriendly and unlikely kind of country. It is a rather barren land. It is in the Arabian peninsula and near a big, old, rocky mountain—a huge pile of rocks that the Bible calls Mount Sinai. Anyway, around this big, old mountain in this scrubby part of the country, here and there were some thin patches of grass and nearby a spring of water or a pond where rain water occasionally gathered. Here this 80-year-old shepherd, by the name of Moses, was feeding his sheep, as he had been doing for forty years.

One day he saw a bush that was on fire. He watched it for a while. The funny thing was that it did not burn up. So he went over to have a look at it. As he got over by the bush, a voice came out of the bush and said, "Moses, take off your shoes because the ground on which you are standing is holy ground." So Moses flipped off his sandals and lifted up his cloak over his face because he was afraid to look upon the presence of God.

And God said to Moses, "Moses, let me tell you something. I have seen the affliction of my people Israel down in Egypt under the strong, cruel hand of Pharaoh, where they have been living as slaves for nearly four hundred years. I have heard their cry and their prayers. I have come down to deliver them and to set them free." "Hooray!" said Moses in his heart. "That is what we have been praying for and looking for, for a long time. Go to it, God, set them free!"

But the next thing God said was, "Moses, come here and I will send you to Pharaoh and you shall set my people free." Moses backed away, saying, "Oh, God, you can't mean me. You can't use me. I'm not the man you want. Go get somebody else." And so Moses started a whole series of arguments with God. "Just look at me. I'm an old man. I can't speak; I'm no man of speech. I don't have the credentials and I don't have the tools to work with."

"Well," said God, "What's that you have in your hand?" "Oh," said Moses, "That's just my shepherd's staff, that's all." God said, "That's all I need. Take and throw it on the ground." And as Moses threw it on the ground, it became a serpent, and Moses became frightened, and he began to run. Then God said, "No, Moses, don't run. Walk over and take it by the tail." So he walked over and took the serpent by the tail and it stretched right up and became a shepherd's staff in his hand again. "That's all you need. Take that staff now and go to Pharaoh."

That staff became his through obedience to the word of God. He took it in the grasp of faith, a rod of redemption, a rod of power, a rod of force. And God worked with Moses by his rod and nothing more. He delivered Israel out of Egypt, brought them across the Red Sea, brought them for forty years through the wilderness right up to the borders of the land of Canaan. God sustained him and took care of him and used him and his shepherd's rod and that was enough for God's purposes.

Now that is just how God goes about it, how Jesus goes about calling and bringing the other sheep in this world into his fold. First, he comes to his church, his people, and he says to us, "All of you are my sheep. You are my flock. Now there are also other sheep all over. Them also I must bring. You come now and I'll send you to them."

The missionary calling begins in this way, but it may not come in the same way to all people, but the elements are the same. God calls and sends people who first of all come to understand something of God's redemptive purpose, his missionary purpose in this world. They come to see the people of this world as Jesus saw them and they see his desire to reach out and call them in. And then, somehow, they hear the Lord Jesus say to them, "Now you come and I will send you to Pharaoh to set my people free."

The normal reaction of most people to God's call is to back away and say, "Lord, that's a good idea, of course, I'm all for your bringing in those other sheep, but would you please go to someone else more eligible and suited for the task?" But somehow when God has picked out a Moses, he can't back away from the call of God. It sticks with him. It persists. And God the Holy Spirit keeps pressing his claim on such a person's life. This is what happens also whenever a congregation experiences the words of Jesus when he says, "The harvest is abundant, but the workers are few. Pray to the Lord of the harvest who will send workers out into the harvest." If we seriously pray that way, it will be no surprise if the Holy Spirit reaches right down into our own company and lays hold on one or another of those in our company and thrusts him out into the harvest.

This is what happened with our mission, the little mission called World Mission Prayer League. There was a group of students in a missions class at one of our Lutheran Bible Institutes. In this class the students came to realize that Jesus has many other sheep and wants to call them into his flock. They saw that. They were burdened about that. They formed a little prayer league and began to pray. For five and a half years they prayed. Then the Lord put his hand on two men in that little prayer group and he said, "Moses, you come now and I'll send you off to South America." When God confirmed this to their hearts, these two men said, "All right, Lord, we will go, but how shall we go? Who can send us? How can this work out?"

And God said to them, "What have you got in your hand?" They answered, "Oh, all we've got is a little prayer group. We call them the Prayer League for South America." "All right," said God, "That's all you need. Use them. Throw it down on the ground, in other words put it at my disposal. Now take it by the tail and walk off to Egypt with it." So they said, "All right, Lord," and they went to the little prayer group and said, "Folks, we've been praying that God would send somebody off. Now God has called us to go and we can't find any way to go. Would you people now be willing to form a little mission and sponsor our going?" So one Sunday afternoon, on a hot August day at a Bible camp on a little lake west of Minneapolis, the little prayer league, which had organized itself into a mission, accepted these two brethren as their first volunteer candidates to go to South America.

A little while later, in a church of which I am a member in Minneapolis, some of us gathered around these two men at a Sunday evening service. We did like the believers did in Antioch, in the thirteenth chapter of Acts, when Paul and Barnabas were called by God for missionary work, and they separated them for the work to which God had called them. And having done this, they sent them forth, and they went on their way. So they started off for South America.

At this time there was a group of fellows, six in all, five of us in fact born and raised in China. While we were in school, we met during our vacations, praying and studying and talking, trying to find out how God wanted us to use our lives in his service. Our attention became focused on Central Asia. It was an area without the gospel, and soon we believed God was calling us to try to penetrate the heart of Asia to bring the good news of Jesus there.

We all went to our church leaders about this. After three long sessions we were told, "Sorry, we cannot undertake something like that." So two of us joined this little prayer group for South America. They took us in and we began to move out towards Asia. And in that way things began. We found that God was asking us to take the staff, the things we had in our hands, and give them up to him, and answer his summons. What we have will be sufficient equipment to get done what he calls us to do. And so we started out.

We had two things in mind especially. One was that we felt we should go to those places where our official church boards did not have mission work. We certainly were not seeking to compete with what our church was doing, but to supplement it. In the second place we felt that we could supplement the foreign mission work of our church by making it possible for lay people, who ordinarily are not qualified to go under our church boards, to serve abroad.

Ordinary Christians who know their Bible, who know the Lord Jesus and walk with him, are able to help others to come to a personal faith in Christ and to instruct them in the faith so that they will gather into groups of believers. They can work happily and effectively in the outlying places. And so we kept praying that God would send workers into his harvest. And God picked out men and women as he did Moses and said to them, "You go. I'll tell you where Pharaoh is, that you might deliver my people in Bolivia, in Ecuador, in Mexico, and here and there in different parts of the world."

There are now about one hundred twenty-five of us; during the last thirty years or more, I think we've been about two hundred fifty altogether who have come and gone to different places. Most of us are lay people. Yes, by far most of us have been lay persons. We came from about fifty different kinds of occupations to join with the little family mission endeavor which has been growing up out of its simple beginnings.

# 10
# Is WMPL a "Faith Mission?"

*Paul's letter in the 50's in reply to a question of the nature of the World Mission Prayer League.*

Dear _____,

In reply to your question as to why we "do not like to be thought of as a faith mission," let me say: I don't think I would put it quite that way. I would rather say we have avoided using that term, and that we have done so for the simple reason that (1) it is not very useful for our purpose, and, ( 2) it is very often the cause for much misunderstanding.

The term is used in different ways by different groups and lacks a clear definition. The name "faith mission" was not chosen or assumed by the missions that have come to be called by this term, but it was given to them by others because of their distinctive policy and practice regarding financial support for their missionaries. That is how it all started, I believe. Since then a multitude of mission organizations and a host of independent missionaries have taken to the title, even though they have developed a wide variety in policies and practices.

Also, because the term "faith mission" has been used quite generally to distinguish those societies that employ missionaries from many denominational backgrounds from those that serve only one denomination, we have felt it best to avoid the term.

Unfortunately, many people think of "faith missions" in a judgmental sort of way. Some feel that the "faith missions" exhibit a greater faith than missions of a different order. And other people feel that the "faith missions" tend to give the impression that only they do their work by real faith and that the denominational missions are of a little lower quality of faith and spiritual power. For this reason too we have felt it best not to use a term that has suffered from such misuse.

We are keenly conscious of the lack and frailty of our faith, and have prayed that the Lord would increase and strengthen our dependence upon him, and we have tried humbly to take the position of looking to the Lord day by day for the supply of what we have needed, grateful for whatever He has provided and by whatever means this has come to us.

I should also mention that during these 20 years that we have been working, we have come to see that to trust God for the supply of our material needs is really the least and easiest part of the work that faith has to accomplish. The preaching and teaching of the Bible, the forming of churches, the training of national converts, the conflict with heathenism and darkness, the maintaining of spiritual life, and the simple matter of entrusting the good tidings of the Church to national Christians—all of this takes strong, steady and vigorous faith. This kind of faith, thank God, is found among Christian workers in all kinds of missions, and this is the sort of faith that really counts and that really gets things done. We have admired it wherever we have seen it and it has been our desire to be "not slothful but followers of those who through faith and patience have inherited the promises" (Hebrews 6:12).

But now I have written enough. Thanks again for your very encouraging letter. May the Lord bless and use you in all that you do for His Kingdom.

Yours in His Fellowship,

*Paul J. Lindell*

# 11
# Mouth and Hands
# Work Together

*Part of a serialized article by Paul in three issues of "Luth-eran World Vision."*

## August, 1965

One notable feature of the Christian movement in the Roman world of 100-500 A.D. was the great development of charitable services. These were given especially to those who were of the household of the faith but they also reached far towards people who were outsiders, even to those who were foes and tormentors of Christians. Harnack, the church historian, writes at length about no less than ten such forms of service, including the care of orphans, widows, prisoners and travelers.

Some of the early records suggest that the churches first found favor and legal recognition from a hostile government as burial clubs. The Emperor Julian (332-363 A.D.), an apostate enemy of Christian faith who tried to restore the old idolatry of Rome, wrote a complaint about the Christians (which really was a compliment to them): "Atheism (by this he meant Christian faith) has been specially advanced through the loving service rendered to strangers and through their care for the burial of the dead. It is a scandal that there is not a single Jew who is a beggar, and that the godless Galileans care not only for their own poor but for ours as well; while those who belong to us look in vain for the help that we should render them."

These were hard times for Christians. They were poor and despised. They were weak and scattered. They were hunted down and destroyed in some places. But so well did their faith and works combine to witness for Christ that they overcame evil with good. Mouth and hands, working faithfully together, outlasted their strongest opponents and many people looking on were persuaded to become Christians.

## 1,500 YEARS LATER

Now take a long leap in your history book. Turn the pages, past the Dark Ages, past the Crusades, past the Reformation and stop a moment in England at about the year 1800 A.D. William Carey, the shoemaker-teacher-preacher-missionary from Nottingham had just sailed with his family for far away India, never to return. In some strange way his example touched off an amazing flood of missionary love and labor that soon covered the world.

In the immediate years that followed most of the major English missionary societies were formed. The very first company of missionaries sent out by one of these missions (The London Missionary Society) included: six carpenters, one shopkeeper, one harness-maker, two tailors, one blacksmith, one cooper, one butcher, two weavers, one hatter, one linen-draper, one gentleman servant, one gardener, one surgeon, one cotton textile manufacturer, two shoemakers, two bricklayers, one cabinetmaker.

These people were commissioned and sent to teach their crafts, arts and trades as they preached the gospel to "uncivilized" people who knew nothing of wearing shoes or hats, nothing of medicines or books, nothing of machines or wages for labor. And in the 165 years that have passed since then many thousands of men and women have left their homes to live and work in a hundred different foreign lands, combining their preaching and hymn singing and praying with all kinds of useful services by which to help needy people all around them. In India alone Christian missionaries have built and operated 250 hospitals with more than 20,000 beds. And wherever they have gone, missionaries have cared for orphans, received the homeless, befriended the blind and cared for the helpless. They have built schools of all kinds. They have produced books and taught people to read. They have worked to improve land and crops, wages and housing, health and social relations.

All of these strong missionary efforts have focused upon three major concerns:

1. A concern to civilize the backward people of the world. "Evangelization" and "civilization" went hand in hand in early missionary thinking, writing and talking. People could easily see the need for both of these in "heathen" lands and who could be better able to take both to them than the missionaries? The only debatable question was which ought to come first. Would it be possible to civilize people unless they were first of all converted to Christ? Or, could "heathen" people understand the Word of God unless they were first of all civilized to some extent? Most missionaries didn't bother to argue about this but went about doing all they could with both evangelizing and civilizing in whatever way they could.

2. A concern for human need. Missionaries were appalled at the poverty, disease, ignorance, filth and degradation they found when they came to their mission fields. People suffered terribly under these disastrous conditions. Misery, distress and heartaches cried for help. Who could think of ignoring these cries? But what could be done? What help could be given? That was the only question.

3. A concern for social righteousness. Wicked, evil, inhuman practices robbed millions of people of happiness, dignity, human rights and worth. Widows were burned alive with the remains of their dead husbands. Little girls had their toes broken and their feet bound and maimed for life. Other girls were trapped in shameful slavery as temple prostitutes. The sale of opium ruined many good men and their fortunes. Millions were oppressed by heartless landlords, unscrupulous money lenders, merciless brigands or unjust rulers. Polygamy made impossible the unity of family life. The slave trade ran like a stinking ulcer in the body of society. Are missionaries to stand by and do nothing to stop these monstrous evils? Can a missionary preach only for the salvation of men's souls and do nothing to redeem their bodies, their minds, their homes and their communities?

These concerns compelled missionaries to be zealous social reformers as well as vigorous evangelists. While they preached with their mouths they labored with their hands to heal, to lift, to help and to bless all who would receive their aid.

## A DISPUTED QUESTION

After a hundred years some missionaries began seriously to question whether church missions should mix evangelizing and church building with all kinds of programs for human social betterment in this world. A running dispute developed which has ever since been going on. Something of this dispute may be seen in almost any missionary journal today and it turns up constantly in missionary conferences and seminars.

Some argue strongly for the necessity of schools, hospitals, health campaigns, literacy programs, agricultural missions and all the other kinds of social service given by missionaries the world over. Others argue just as strongly that Christian missions should leave these matters alone and that missionaries should stick fast to their divine mission of preaching the gospel and of persuading men to be reconciled to God. Especially in the present day when it has become axiomatic for governments to assume responsibility and care for the needs of the poor and the helpless there is little practical reason for missionaries to be sidetracked from their gospel ministry to carry the burdens of mundane life in the communities around them.

Consider first the case **for** Christian social services in missionary work. Out of all the arguments that are advanced to support missionary involvement in medical, education, agricultural and other kinds of programs let me list very simply the following considerations:

1—**The example of Jesus and the Apostles.** During his public ministry Jesus went about preaching and healing, "doing good." At the start he announced his program in the words of Isaiah: "The Spirit of the Lord is upon me, because he has anointed me to preach good news to the poor. He has sent me to proclaim release to the captives and recovering of sight to the blind, and to set at liberty those who are oppressed." Later on he sent his disciples throughout the towns and villages to do the same. This pattern and purpose of helping and delivering people in their distresses has never been changed in the Christian tradition. In holding out our hands to the helpless and to those in need we do as our Lord has done.

2— **Compassion demands it.** "Jesus had compassion on them and healed their sick" (Matthew 14:14). This was said over and over again about him in the New Testament Gospels. It is the nature of love to "bear the infirmities of the weak and not to please yourself." A Christian must be one who cares, and cares enough to make right what he sees to be wrong, make good what he sees to be bad, make well what he sees to be ill, and make strong what he sees to be weak. "But if any one has this world's goods and sees his brother in need, yet closes his heart against him, how does God's love abide in him? Little children, let us not love in word or speech but in deed and truth" (1 John 3:17).

3—**We serve God by serving others.** God loves the poor and is gracious to all that are oppressed. The Psalms are full of such expressions about God and his unending mercy. And when we help the helpless and give aid to people who need loving care in the name of Christ, the Lord regards this as a service to himself. This is certainly the plain meaning of that awesome passage in Matthew 25:31-46, which describes the coming of the Son of Man in his glory on the last day with all his angels to judge the nations of the world that are gathered before him. He will then say to those who have been placed at his right hand, "I was hungry and you gave me food, I was thirsty and you gave me drink, I was a stranger and you welcomed me in, I was in prison and you came to me.... Truly, I say to you, as you did it to one of the least of these my brethren, you did it to me."

4—**It is of the nature of true faith to do good works.** They go together and cannot be divorced. Works of love and help to others are the evidence of genuine and living faith in Christ as the Savior and Lord over all. "If a brother or sister is ill-clad and in lack of daily food and one of you says to him, 'Go in peace, be warmed and filled,' without giving them the things needed for the body, what does it profit? So faith by itself, if it have no works, is dead" (James 2:16-17).

**5—Redemption in Christ is for the whole man, body, soul and spirit.** People are made in the image of God to live and walk as sons and daughters of the Most High God. And though they have fallen from this glorious position they have been "ransomed with the precious blood of Christ" from the futile ways of this world. Each person thus possesses a dignity and worth in the sight of God that surpasses anything else in this world. And the missionary aim must be to recover men so completely that each one may be brought to love and serve God "with all his heart, and with all his soul, and with all his mind, and with all his strength." This means that we must give careful attention to the whole man to help him to live wholly for God in all the relationships of his life.

**6—It is a rightful duty to give help to others.** God tells us plainly that we are to do this. John the Baptist declared to his hearers, "He who has two coats, let him share with him who has none; and he who has food, let him do likewise" (Luke 3:11). Saint Paul told the church in Rome, "Let each of us please his neighbor for his good, to edify him. For Christ did not please himself" (Romans 15:1-3). And our Lord Jesus said, after telling the story of the Good Samaritan to explain who is to be regarded as our neighbor, "Go and do likewise." And then John the Apostle declares simply, "He who does good is of God" (3 John:11).

**7—Good works help to build friendly relations with non-Christians.** There is so often a gulf of hostility and suspicion between Christians and the unbelieving community. But we are to count no man as our enemy. We are to strive for peace with all men. Of all people in this world we should be the first to hold out the hand of peace and good will to our neighbors. And the clearest expression of Christian concern for the good of others, even for those most opposed to us, may be seen in the way we work to help those who are in trouble and need.

8—**Good works open the way for evangelism.** Some
people will let us work good with our hands before they will
let us speak the good things of the gospel with our mouths.
The walls of suspicion, prejudice, hatred and opposition have
many times been broken down by gentle deeds of love and
goodness so that a way could be prepared for the coming of the
Word of Life. "Don't you know," asks the Apostle Paul, "that
the goodness of God is meant to lead you to repentance?"
(Romans 2:4). And surely this must include the goodness of
God by the hands of his messengers and servants as much as
his goodness in bestowing gifts of rain and sunshine, crops
and fruits, health and well-being upon all people.

9—**Social services aid the churches, which are so often
small and weak, as they confront an unfriendly world
around them.** Hospitals and schools and other social programs give the churches a respected status in the community.
They also help to provide trained leaders both for the church
work and for the civil institutions. They provide Christians
with a big opportunity to give a strong witness for Christ by
deeds as well as by words to their unconverted neighbors.
"Let your light so shine before men that they may see your
good works and give glory to your Father who is in heaven"
(Matthew 5:16).

10—**Social services introduce the rule of Christ into
many secular phases of community life.** This is a good way
to work "salt" into the earth, as Jesus put it. The coming of
God's Kingdom into man's affairs means that selfishness,
pride, hatred and dishonesty should be replaced with love,
truth, humility and righteousness. What a glorious prospect!
What a challenging vision and call to work for the salvation
of man and the revolution of his life so as to bring everything
into submission to Christ, "Be not overcome by evil, but
overcome evil with good" (Romans 12:21).

11—**The skills and knowledge we have are gifts from
God.** If God's good gifts are hoarded or used selfishly they will
soon be lost or become a curse to us. "Freely you received,"
said Jesus to his disciples, "freely give." "Love your enemies,

and do good, and lend, expecting nothing in return; and your reward will be great, and you will be sons of the Most High; for he is kind to the ungrateful and the selfish. Be merciful, even as your father is merciful" (Luke 6:35-36).

These are some of the reasons that have moved Christian missionaries to work for the material, physical, mental and social good of any and all of the people among whom they live and minister. Love is ingenious, resourceful, always doing and never tired. And Christian love has produced an amazing variety of good works in the name of Christ all across the world to share with others all the good things that are ours in Christ.

# September, 1965

Social services have become so commonly a regular part of missionary work that it would be hard to imagine what missionaries would do without them. And yet there is another side to it. We do not need to listen to outside critics to find this out because some of the very best missionaries have earnestly warned against harmful dangers that lie hidden in all of this good effort.

They do not say that Christians should ignore the needs of men, or that Christians should be concerned only with spiritual matters and not with physical, material and secular affairs. Indeed, Christians should be in the forefront and should lead the way in caring for the orphan, the widow, the leper, the weak and feeble, the ignorant, the poor, the outcast, the lawbreaker, the laborer and all who are in any way helpless, neglected or suffering.

But, they say, Christians should do this as members of the community, together with their fellow-citizens, and not as official missionaries sent and employed to do this under their own mission or church organizations and under the control of these organizations. The distinction is important and the reasons for thinking this way are weighty. Consider some of them:

1—**Care for the body tends to crowd out care for the soul.**
Complaints about this often appear in the published diaries
of many well-known missionaries. The heavy demands of
institutional work have robbed much time that should have
been given to preaching the gospel, teaching and explaining
the Bible or helping people with spiritual problems.

When times of shortage come in mission resources, evangelism is squeezed out and workers and funds are pushed into
keeping the social service institutions going. It is easier to
close down meetings, Bible classes, radio programs, Sunday
schools and door-to-door visitation than it is to shut down
school rooms, hospital wards, printing presses or administrative offices. The mission is under stronger obligation to the
community to continue social services, or at least the demands of the community are stronger for these, and so the
mission draws in all of its personnel and funds to maintain
these. And evangelism must wait for a favorable time to get
started again.

2—**Social work yields little spiritual fruit as compared
with evangelism and Bible teaching.** Schools, medical
work and other service programs are expensive and give little
in return for building up the life of the Church. If the primary
object of missions is the conversion of unbelievers and the
growth of the Christian Church then the very best investment
of the missionary dollar and of the missionary's effort to reach
this objective is in evangelism and in Bible teaching.

Responsible stewardship should therefore give top priority
to evangelism and Bible teaching and never allow any other
activity or interest to crowd in upon this. But this unfortunately is not the case. In fact there are some places where
large amounts of missionary money are used just to ease the
physical conditions of people and nothing is done to put the
Word of God into the hands or into the ears of the people, as
with the Muslim Arab refugees in Jordan.

3—**Social services often give a very wrong impression of
Christianity when they are conducted by Christian missions.** Some think that it must be a very expensive and costly
religion to have so many buildings, offices, employees and

activities. A well-groomed Sikh on a train in India told me that he thought that Christianity (judging by the Christian missionary program in India) was a religion that sought to make life on earth more pleasant and worthwhile for people. It was a way of making friends with all people in the world more than a way of making friends with God.

Others get the impression that the propagation of Christianity can be carried out only by professionals and by people with high degrees and specialized talents in some useful human art. Still others see missions as a form of western imperialism, a handmaid of western civilization and that through its institutions the Christian mission is fastening foreign domination and foreign patterns of living upon the people it pretends to serve. This is what the institutions make it look like to some people.

**4—Social service institutions hinder development of local indigenous churches.** It does this in at least three ways. First, by developing costly institutions that poor churches can never take over and maintain. And the idea of missions is to turn over their work to the local churches as soon as possible. Second, costly institutions hinder and discourage stewardship and evangelism. They strengthen the idea that missions are obliged to support converts and their churches since missionaries came and started all of this. Third, costly institutions with their large budgets give a wide opportunity for the ugly play of power politics in the life of churches. Examples of this can be seen all over the world today.

**5—Christian institutions become secularized so quickly, with only a thin veneer of Christian appearance on the outside.** Pagan students fill the classrooms of Christian schools. Non-Christians are taken onto the staffs of every kind of mission institution. Christian meetings and services of a spiritual nature are kept at a minimum. Policies come to be determined by financial needs or by the opinion pressure of non-Christians connected with the institutions rather than by the aims of the Christian mission. Bit by bit the control slips out of the hands of Christians and more and more "the world" takes over.

A sad and humiliating example of the miscarriage of a missionary project may be seen in Gordon College at Khartum in Africa. Founded and built with funds contributed by Christians in England to provide Christian education in Africa, the college has been gradually turned into a center of Muslim teaching and influence. Small compromising steps develop a trend that cannot be stopped or reversed and in time the whole thing is "sold down the river" to secular interest. But why look to Africa? The same thing has happened to great Christian colleges in our own country.

**6—Nowhere in the New Testament do we get the idea that the Church is called or sent to meet the human needs of men outside the fellowship of the Church.** To alleviate suffering, to improve social conditions, to help people in need is in truth the rightful concern and duty of each Christian as a member of his community. But this is not the job of the Church or of any mission of the Church. The early New Testament Church did what it could to care for the needs of its own members, as brothers and sisters do in a family, but they never expressed any feeling that the Church should organize programs for bringing relief of any kind to those outside the Christian community.

**7—Social service institutions easily become the private preserve of professionals and self-righteous professionalism can work at ruinous cross-purposes to Christian missions.** One danger is that efficiency becomes more important than people. Make people fit into the program of the institution rather than fit the program to the needs of the people.

In 1949 there were 10,000 beggars on the streets of Kunming in West China. A missionary lady doctor who had been forced out of North China by the advancing Communist armies came to wait at Kunming until she could return to her post. When other missionaries asked her to help them do something for the mobs of beggars, she refused. She was trained to run a hospital, she said, and not to hand out pills at some sidewalk dispensary to beggars. If she couldn't run a proper hospital she would rather sit on her hands and do nothing. Meanwhile the beggars could go to the dogs.

A second danger with professionalism is that the ordinary Christian is led to feel that he can help others only by proxy, by letting the hired professionals do it for him. He doesn't have to be personally involved. Since only experts can help others, this lets him off. This feeling can effectively choke off any impulse in the churches to rise up and help others with just the simple things that they have. And that would be tragic.

A third danger with professionalism is that service may be changed from the ministry of a servant to become the benevolent bestowal of a benefactor (a kind of Santa Claus). Servants work at the beck and call of others, usually the same people, all the time, and the service is more or less taken for granted. This was what Saint Paul said about himself: "We are your servants for Jesus' sake." But benefactors serve when and where and how and whom they please. This is a kind of service that is foreign to the New Testament.

8—Social services tend to be confused with preaching the gospel. This is a very serious theological objection. Sometimes we hear about ministering the gospel through medicine, or through the school classroom, or through sports activities, or agricultural programs. Here the point of contact for the salvation of lost sinners is the physical help received rather than the proclamation of the good news. It takes the place of the preached Word of God, as if the gospel somehow needed help from the good deeds done by men to be effective in bringing people to repentance and faith. The gospel is itself and alone the power of God unto salvation to every one that believes, and it begs help from no other source to accomplish its mission. To do any mixing and jumbling here would be treason to the Word of God and it would cheat men out of hearing the gospel in truth and purity.

9—Christian service programs are often confused with humanism. Where is the difference? The Red Cross, the Rockefeller Foundation, the USOM and other government programs are all spoken of as "missions" around the world. They, together with the welfare programs of the newly independent nations, all serve the commonly recognized needs of men. It has become axiomatic that it is the business of government to heal the sick, teach the unlearned, employ the idle, improve farm production, and provide the means to make life secure, happy and meaningful. And all of this is based on a rather universal attitude that asserts the dignity and worth of man and his capacity for self-realization through cooperative programs of social uplift.

How is this different from what Christian missions are doing? It might be pointed out that these secular programs put so much emphasis on human welfare and social reform that they give ultimate value to what is only temporal and passing away, while Christian missionary services seek to fit men not only for this life but also the life which is to come. But many people haven't looked closely enough to see this profound difference. It may also be that missionary welfare services have been hiding their light under a bushel.

10—**Good deeds done in a big, organized way make men the center of attention and attraction.** Those who manage the service become the objects of praise and adulation. Jesus sternly warns against this (Matthew 6:1-4) and says that our alms should be given in secret, where our left hand does not know what our right hand is doing. In contrast to this, Jesus said in Matthew 5:14-16 that we are to let our light shine before men. This must refer to our calling to bring the light of the gospel to all the world ("you are the light of the world"). Thus, good deeds of help are to be done "in secret," God-ward. But to let the light shine is a public open ministry, man-ward. This emphatic distinction is blurred when missions go in for large, public, social service institutions.

11—**Social service institutions generate secular power.** Missionaries and their institutions become employers, consumers and owners of property in the community. This puts them in positions of influence and power in the whole complex of competing interest groups or people in society. They become important to the governing officials, to the bankers and tradesmen, to job seekers and to all who look for opportunities to advance their own interest. They gain this importance not from the message they preach but from the secular stature they have gained by their buildings, organization, programs, money and skilled people in their employ.

This is an evangelistic liability. People who respond to the Christian message because it is delivered by a "power" in the community become "rice Christians." People who join the Christian Church because of the personal advantages they derive (better status, schooling, jobs or contracts, to marry a fine wife, to get political backing, etc.) are like the man who built his house upon the sand. The first good rainstorm washes them right out!

You can always evangelize from a position of weakness, but you can never rightly and effectively do it from a position of worldly strength. It is when we are weak that we are truly strong. God's working power is made perfect in weakness.

See our Lord Jesus coming to redeem the world in great weakness, in deep poverty ("no place to lay his head") and going about in the form of a servant. See our Lord sending his disciples to evangelize and telling them: "Take no gold, nor silver, nor copper in your belts, no bag for your journey, nor two tunics, nor sandals, nor a staff. Preach as you go, saying, 'The kingdom of heaven is at hand.' Heal the sick, raise the dead, cleanse lepers, cast out demons. You received without pay, give without pay." To build up positions of secular power and influence in any community while working along these lines would be an impossibility. Perhaps that was just the point. Perhaps Jesus laid out a pattern of ministry for his disciples that would keep them clear of any such tendency.

The message would win its way into men's hearts by way of conviction and faith. "For the kingdom of God does not mean food and drink, but righteousness and peace and joy in the Holy Spirit."

These are some of the arguments raised in opposition to the vast array of charitable institutions that have been built up by missionaries in a hundred lands across the world. Earnest and thoughtful missionaries who have themselves worked zealously to build up these "power structures of mercy" have seen how they hinder and obstruct the primary work of evangelism and church building and in their hearts they have backed away from them.

To show mercy and to aid the needy is undeniably right. It must be done. Christians should press for this. But to do it in such a way that the mission or the church becomes a political factor and a secular force in the community is wrong. It shackles evangelism. It misrepresents the evangelist. It beclouds the gospel.

But the institutions are there and in most places they are flourishing. Millions upon millions of dollars have been invested in them. Many thousands of skilled and highly trained missionaries are working all the time to make them stronger, bigger and better. What then shall be done with them?

And the simple answer is: get rid of them! Give them away. Find ways for the community to take them over. It may be hard to do this. It may take a long time. But aim for this, pursue this aim and don't for a minute look back.

In a few instances where the majority of missionaries in a missionary society have been convinced by this line of thought they have shut down any schools or hospitals they may have had and put their work on a straight program of evangelism. In other places, as in Ceylon, missions and churches have been helped to this by the government when all social institutions have been taken over by the state.

And the day may not be far off when governments all over the world will require that all such institutions be handed over to the state. This will be a great loss in money and status to missions and churches. It will make the Christian Church look weak and poor and of no account.

But it could be also the beginning of a new day for Christian missions. It can bring a new and startling rediscovery of the strange paradox uttered by Saint Paul when he said: "But the Lord said to me, 'My grace is sufficient for you, for my power is made perfect in weakness.' I will all the more gladly boast of my weaknesses, that the power of Christ may rest upon me. For the sake of Christ, then, I am content with weaknesses, insults, hardships, persecutions and calamities; for when I am weak, then I am strong."

Meanwhile thousands of social services of one kind or another are being maintained by missions and churches everywhere. New ones are being started right along. There are undoubtedly many more missionaries going abroad to work in social service institutions than to work exclusively as evangelists or to concentrate on teaching and preaching the Word of God.

But must Christian missions be all mouth and no hands— all preaching and no helpful service to people? Cannot mouth and hand work together? Indeed, if the Christian Church be thought of as a body, it would be badly crippled unless it could use both hands and voice to fulfill its calling from God to the unconverted people of the world.

# January, 1966

A vast amount of money and high percentage of the missionary force of workers are employed in social services. These services include a variety of medical work (hospitals, dispensaries, clinics, mobile units), schools of different kinds, industrial and agricultural projects, community social centers, cooperatives, relief programs for the poor and for refugees who have suffered loss from floods, disasters and political upheavals.

There is some disagreement in missionary thinking about the right place and function of all of this effort in the ministry of Christian missions. We have considered briefly before some of the arguments that are offered in support of such social services in missions. And we have also looked at the case against conducting all kinds of humanitarian work through the agencies of church missions. Some think that missionaries should stick strictly to preaching and teaching the Word of God and to evangelism and church building.

In our experience as a missionary fellowship we have found opportunity to do both, and to do them together, hand in hand —to preach and teach the life-giving Word of God, and at the same time to help people with their temporal needs. We do this not just because there are opportunities to do so, but because we believe they go together. Take a simple illustration:

*It was three o'clock P.M., the mid-afternoon hour of prayer in Jerusalem. Peter and John went to the temple to pray and at the gate they saw a poor man sitting beside the entrance with his hand outstretched to receive alms. "Look at us," said Peter. The beggar stared intently, expecting to receive a coin. "I do not have silver and gold," Peter declared, "but I give you what I have; in the name of Jesus Christ of Nazareth, walk!" And Peter took him by the right hand and raised him up. Immediately his feet and ankles were made strong and he ran and leaped and praised God in the court of the temple (Acts 3:6-7).*

This man is the world. Look through him and you see the whole world of troubled people, millions upon millions of them. They are all individuals, like this one man. Their troubles are personal. Unless the masses of the world's people can be seen and helped one by one they will appear a blur, out of focus. And unless our missionary ministry can save and help the one man in his troubles it will be ineffective for the millions. The test of our work is with the man at the gate. If we fail to help him there we will likely fail to help the city, or the nation.

This man cannot hide his troubles. He is crippled, has been so from his birth (health problem). He is poor, unemployed and dependent (economic problem). He is a beggar. No one invites him to tea. No one stops to chat with him about politics, or sports or even the weather (social problem).

"I do not have silver or gold," Peter told him as he looked down at him with all his problems. Without money Peter could do little or nothing about the man's economic problem. Furthermore, being an "unlearned" and "common" man and one who belonged to a despised and persecuted minority group in the city, Peter did not have much of a solution to his man's social problem either.

Similarly, we know that as Christian missionaries we do not have some magical formula, some divine cure, or some inspired plan for meeting and resolving the world's temporal problems. These ills have been with the human family from the very beginning and will be with us till the last day. They become more complex, more pressing and seemingly more insoluble with every passing season.

Billions and billions of dollars are spent every year by

governments, private agencies and individuals to find solutions for the sorrows of mankind. Skilled and able people give the best of their lives to research, experimentation and applied programs in the hope of ridding the world of poverty, illness, ignorance, conflict and insecurity. But no one yet has the prescription that will cure, or the recipe that will build up the good life for all.

And as missionaries we do not claim or pretend to have it either. When we go to Bolivia, or Nepal, or anywhere else, we do not imagine that we bring either the resources or the "know-how" for remaking society so that the poor lame man's troubles will be no more. But if this be so, what then do we have to give?

"I give you what I have," said Peter. And thereupon he gave him four things:

1— **The Name of Jesus.** "In the name of Jesus, walk!" Not a formula. Not a ritual. Not a program. Not a theological system. Not an organization. Not even a spiritual experience. But he gave him a name—Jesus, Savior! "Hope of earth and joy of heaven."

This name is the treasure, the gift of God, given for the salvation of all the people. We are commissioned to bear to others the good news that Jesus Christ is the Lamb of God who takes away the sin of the world. Our first and foremost calling is to "preach the unsearchable riches of Christ." For, as Peter declared to the council of the rulers on the following day, "there is salvation in no one else, for there is no other name under heaven given among men by which we must be saved" (Acts 4:12).

2—**Faith in the Name of Jesus.** Note how Peter expressed this to the people who crowded around them: "And his name, by faith in his name, has made this man strong whom you see and know; and the faith which is in Jesus has given the man this perfect health in the presence of you all."

The faiths by which men live are at best only drifting anchors. They do not hold in the storms of life. How hard it is to keep confidence and trust in gods, in ideologies, in governments, in people, in money, in institutions, in science.

They fail us regularly. They are forever changing, or decaying, or even disappearing.

I sat one day in the doorway of a little shop in West China while the old storekeeper explained the loss of his faith to me. The war had upset his orderly world. The old foundations were broken up. The rug had been pulled out from under his feet. "Now long is no longer long," he explained. "Short is no longer short. High is no longer high. Wide is no longer wide. And who knows," he said with a deep sigh, "maybe there aren't even any gods! Ah, it makes my head ache."

Now when the bottom is dropping out of life for people, we bring faith and trust in the name of Jesus. We know him and are convinced that he is able to save unto the uttermost all who come to him. Let come what may, let life and the world and death bring on their worst, we need not fear— "for tribulation, or distress, or persecution, or famine, or nakedness, or peril, or sword shall never separate us from the love of Christ. No, in all these things we are more than conquerors through him that loved us" (Romans 8:35-39).

It is this faith and trust in Jesus Christ that we have to give to the bewildered and lost world, to every single person in it.

3— **The Right Hand of Help.** "And Peter took him by the right hand and raised him up; and immediately his feet and ankles were made strong."

While preaching the matchless name of Jesus and sharing our faith and trust in him, we cannot keep our hands in our pockets. If we have any skills, any strength, any knowledge, any tools in our hands we give these too in the name of Jesus to the man at the gate. By any and all means at our disposal we try to reach out and take him by the right hand and lift him up.

We can lift him physically by medical work and by prayer for his healing. We can lift him economically by helping him to farm better, to learn a trade or to manage his affairs to better profit. We can lift him mentally by giving him what we have of the arts and sciences. We can lift him socially by being his friends and by identifying ourselves with him in his needs and aspirations.

We can do this privately in some instances. We can do this

by our own mission agencies in other situations. And there are some places where we can work with community and government programs to lift the man at the gate to his feet.

But we try to do this in the name of Jesus. It is truly a blessing if the man can get to his feet and never go begging as a cripple again. But we are not fully satisfied until the man can run and leap and praise God in the courts of the temple! Healing and restoration is not complete until a man loves and serves the Lord with all his heart, his soul, his mind and his strength. And only as we hold out our hands by the name of Jesus can we lift crippled people to that fullness of life.

4—"He Clung to Peter and John." That night when the apostles were arrested and put in custody for their public preaching, the healed man went to jail with them. And the next day, when they were brought for a hearing before the council of rulers, he stood right there beside them. They were his friends—indeed, his brothers. He had joined their company.

Thus Peter and John gave him a welcome into the company of the redeemed. They put out their hands and drew him into the household of God, into the family of God's people, into the Church of our Lord Jesus Christ.

We hold it to be our calling to follow this apostolic pattern and example, to "preach Jesus Christ as Lord, with ourselves as your servants for Jesus' sake" (2 Corinthians 4:5). And we steadfastly believe that as we preach Jesus Christ as Savior and Lord, and as we hold out our hands in his name to lift men to their feet, the Holy Spirit will save and enable people to rise up in new life and power to do his will and to praise his name.

# 12

# Tools to Work With

*This article appeared in the May 1966 "Fellow Workers."*

Our mission, like most missions around the world, has undertaken a variety of projects on our different fields. These projects are not ends in themselves but are the means we use to reach our desired goals. In other words, they are our working tools.

When we send missionaries to other lands our first concern as a mission, quite rightly and naturally, is for their support and maintenance. They will need funds for their travel to their assigned fields of work. They must have houses to live in, food to eat and clothes to wear. They ought to have household furniture and equipment, some means for travel and a way to educate their children. If they get sick we must help them to recover health. If they suffer loss from theft, fire or disaster we are bound to help them make up these losses. If they are expelled because of war or unfriendliness we are pledged to bring them home or shift them to other areas where they can continue working.

These are basic, elementary concerns. Essential to missionary work is the missionary. If any missionary work is to be done the missionary himself must be sent, supported and maintained, for he is the worker.

But beyond this it is equally important to fit the workman with good and useful tools. To be sure, in some things he can work with his bare hands. But there are limits to this. His work and efforts may be greatly extended and his usefulness multiplied by having suitable tools to work with. Ask any carpenter, engineer, cook, teacher or scientist if this isn't true in his line of work. And it is no less true when it comes to the work of the missionary.

### PRIMARY TOOLS

Any workman, to do his job well, must start out with a certain amount of knowledge and skill. There is no substitute for this. Without this he will blunder, mess up his work and waste time and material.

For our missionaries we underscore four kinds of basic knowledge as being essential to any useful missionary work.

1—**A Knowledge of Christianity.** This means a good grasp of the contents of the Bible so that one is at home in the Old and New Testaments, familiar with the hundreds of people who move around in its pages and acquainted with the history and events that form the framework of the Bible narrative.

This also means a good understanding of the doctrines and teachings of the Bible. The Bible is a revelation from God. It provides a store of spiritual knowledge which we would otherwise be without. The Bible interprets the events it records and reveals the hand and the thoughts of God in relation to these events. It gathers up the words of God and the faith of believers concerning God and his salvation. Anyone who aims to bring other men out of darkness and into God's marvelous light must be himself a convert and must know "sound doctrine."

And since the Bible nowhere portrays Christianity apart from the Church, the missionary better be one who knows and understands the Church, one who loves and lives in the fellowship of the Church, and one who is ready to share the burdens, the trials and the ministry of the Church.

2—**A Knowledge of How to Propagate Christian Faith.** The mission of the Christian Church is not to influence or to uplift people in a vague and general sort of way. Nor is it just to improve the living conditions and behavior patterns of people so that life will somehow be "more meaningful" (whatever that means!). Some do mistakenly think so. A gentleman told me in India that he understood that the purpose of Christian missions is to make the world a more comfortable place for men to live in.

But Saint Paul says that our objective is to "persuade men," to "turn them from darkness to light and from the power of Satan to God." This means, pure and simple, to win them over from one side to another, to get them to change their minds and to bow their knees to the absolute lordship of Jesus Christ.

It is a mistake to think that human society will be somehow redeemed by social action, that by altering man's environment we will somehow transform the heart and life of people and bring all mankind into the kingdom of God. Clearly, the Bible shows that to redeem human society and to eradicate some of its prevailing ills men and women must be saved from their sins and be transformed in nature by the Holy Spirit.

God's part in this transformation is to give repentance, faith and a new heart and life to sinners who turn to him for mercy and grace. Our part, appointed to us by God, is to "persuade men" by preaching the gospel.

Saint Paul set the example of this in his own missionary ministry. We follow him through the book of Acts and in his letters—arguing, explaining, convincing, and pleading persuasively—trying to prevail upon people to believe something which they did not previously believe and to do something they have never before done.

If this is what missionaries are called to do then they must gain both the knowledge and the skill to win spiritual conquests in the minds and hearts of people who are outside of Christ's kingdom. And this is perhaps all the more true now today, when the idea of persuading people to change their religion is very much frowned upon in our tolerant age. Even many church people will tell you that we must respect the opinions (and especially the religious opinions and beliefs) of others. Their beliefs are as good as ours and they are every bit as sincere as we are. So it is no business of ours to intrude into their private lives and to interfere with what they believe to be true and right.

But whatever people say, we hold it to be our calling to persuade men to forsake their idols, their superstitions, their falsehoods, their selfish living and their sins and to turn to Christ that they might be saved. And we therefore urge prospective missionaries to learn well this indispensable art of persuading men and teaching them to obey all that Christ has commanded us.

3—**The Knowledge of How to Live in the World.** Missionaries must somehow mix and merge into the life of the community where they go to live. They must share in the burdens and cares, and hopes and dreams of their neighbors. Life, daily life, is a composition of toil and suffering, laughter and singing, learning and doing, success and failure. The village or town, and even the great city, is a cluster of homes, shops, offices, markets, temples, schools, theatres, cafes, inns and depots. This is where people are born, where they grow up and live, where they weaken with age and die. This is where people take the raw products of life and fashion them into what men call treasure, culture and heritage.

Into this sort of world Jesus came, to seek and to save people who are lost. But he did not camp outside of town. He moved right in. He became a carpenter and made doors and windows, benches and tables, and added his creative bit to the life of the community. He ate and drank at weddings. He taught and preached in the streets and markets. He wept with sorrow at the graveside with all the others. His kingdom did not conscript men away from their homes and out of their jobs and communities. Not at all. He brought his rule into the daily life of people right where they lived and they brought their time and strength, their thoughts and their skills into captivity to serve him.

"As the Father has sent me," said Jesus to his followers, "so I have sent you." And one idea that surely is included in this matchless expression is the idea that as Jesus came to share the daily life of people in his community so his missionaries are to enter into and share the life of those to whom he sends them.

But to do this one needs to cultivate some useful skill or art that will contribute something of help and value to the community. Many kinds of service have proven to be very useful and helpful in missionary work. And we feel that it is important that missionaries should find some helpful employment and gain knowledge and skill in it before going abroad—whether this be as a teacher, nurse, doctor, farmer, preacher, builder, technician, secretary, athlete or engineer, etc.

4—**A Knowledge of Foreign Languages**, and particularly fluency in the language the missionary must use where he is to live and work. This ought to be self-evident to anyone. Without being able to understand and to speak understand–ably with people a missionary is crippled and half paralyzed at best.

Some languages can be learned at schools and universities. But to teach other languages to new missionaries, missions often cooperate with each other in setting up language training courses. This is possible where a language enjoys a wide range of usage. But in many areas where there are multiple languages, the missionary must hunt and pick up his words as a hen scratches and pecks all around the barnyard for each seed or kernel of corn.

Language is a tool that needs constant sharpening. If, as we say, our job is to "persuade men," then we have to use words and languages to do this. The message, to be persuasive and convincing, must be understood. The words must be right, the accent must be familiar and the impulses of the heart must flow freely. If this tool is dull or blunt, or if the workman is unskilled with it, few people will be persuaded.

## SECONDARY TOOLS—PROJECTS

In a short time after coming to a mission field the missionary is sure to begin projects of one kind or another. For a time he may scatter his words and efforts, much as the old-time farmer did with his seed when he took it by the fistful from the bag at his side and flung it broadcast all over the ground.

But soon things come into a better focus for the missionary and he thinks of ways to direct his work to better purpose, to meet needs that exist and to conserve the gains that he has made. Others come to work with him and their labors will be productive and fruitful if they can hitch up and pull together on some program. Thus and so they agree to certain projects and take places of responsibility for them.

Some projects begin almost by accident, or at least without much forethought and design. A missionary woman, for example, opens her door to the street one morning and finds at the threshold an abandoned baby girl wrapped in only a thin bit of cloth. She takes the baby in and bathes, feeds and clothes her. No one comes to claim the infant and no one can be persuaded to care for it. A month later a second baby finds its way into her arms, and thus she has the start of an orphanage.

I wonder how many of the orphanages run by Christian missions around the world just happened to begin in some such way as this. Perhaps most of them. And some have grown to be very large, caring for many hundreds and even thousands of homeless children.

Mission projects fall into three general classes, judging by the purposes they serve.

**1—The first class would cover those projects that relate to evangelism.** A good example is the Evangelism in Depth program in Bolivia last year. In this program our mission joined hands with all of the other Evangelicals in Bolivia to cover the entire country with the gospel in the course of one year. There were meetings everywhere, large and small. There was a house-to-house visitation by Christians to give a witness for the Lord. Gospel literature, especially prepared for the campaign, was everywhere distributed. Every congregation was fully mobilized to take a full part. Gifts were gathered up to meet the expenses for publicity, for rent of auditoriums, for radio time, for speakers, for travel, for literature, etc. I believe that the contribution from our Mission amounted to about $1,500.

Another example is the radio station we plan to build in Bolivia. We have bought the land where the station is to stand. We have accepted the appointed two families who will be involved with setting up the station and running it. The transmitter has been built and is waiting to be shipped from Iowa to the lowland site in Bolivia where it will broadcast the gospel. We are working now to get a permit for the station from the government. A studio building will have to be built, a diesel power plant will have to be set up and an antenna will have to be erected before we can begin to broadcast. We will have to have tape recorders and other equipment too that are essential to this project. These are only some of the physical structures and furniture that make broadcasting possible.

In addition to this there is of course the whole business of making programs, gathering a library of tapes and keeping in touch with the listening audience.

We have already received and invested several thousand dollars in this project and it will take much more before it is on its feet. But we do trust that the Lord will give us the supporting help of many friends who will want to share in this evangelistic venture with their gifts.

**2—A second kind of project relates to church building.** When people hear and respond to the gospel, when they turn in faith to the Savior and together worship him, there you have a church or congregation. The fellowship may be small and weak. It will need help and encouragement.

One very helpful way to strengthen the churches is to develop Bible training schools where men and women can be helped to become firm in faith and able teachers of the Word of God. We have tried to do this in all of our fields. In Bolivia and India the Bible schools have been well established now for some years. The Bible school in Pakistan is well on the way. In Ecuador a Bible school has had a good beginning and we hope for growth and development.

The Mission in Bolivia came to believe that by helping to build a good sizable church building in La Paz the whole Lutheran Church in the country would be strengthened and encouraged. So we have been gathering funds for this and a beginning has been made in the building. The base, the arches and the roof. And now the building fund is exhausted. To complete the plan and to get all of the building ready for use, we shall need another $15,000. For this we are praying and we trust that the Lord will provide this in good time for this project.

The school at Risalpur in West Pakistan helps to strengthen the churches by teaching and training the children of Christian families. In the strong Muslim society in which they live many of these children would have little opportunity to attend school. And those who could attend might easily be swallowed up by Islam.

This school should be enlarged to include a high school. And it can be made far more effective by providing a boarding department so that boys and girls from churches in the whole frontier area can come and attend a Christian school all through the grades and high school. We hope that it will not be long until these improvements can be made. The land is there on which to build. We have the money to sink a tube well so that there will be no shortage of water (a problem in this region). And we have good hope of being able to get a permit to build the necessary buildings for classes, dormitories and staff dwellings.

3—**A third class of project is directed to the needs of the community.** For example, the Mission Hospital at Tank in West Pakistan ministers to thousands of sick people who come with their ailments and illnesses from not only the immediate community by from as far as the distant hills of Afghanistan.

We are in the midst of a re-development program at this hospital. We received nearly $50,000 from the Bread For the World program in Germany, through the Lutheran World Federation, for the first phase of this project. This included a residence for nurses, a new water supply system, a combined surgery-recovery section in the hospital, a good wall to enclose a part of the hospital compound and some servants' dwellings.

A second phase of this development program has now been approved and we expect further gifts of nearly $70,000. When this is completed there will be yet a third phase, the provision of a mobile unit to take dispensary services to surrounding villages.

Another example of medical projects in which we are involved is the mission hospital in Kathmandu, Nepal. For some years now this hospital has been housed in a couple of old palace buildings, residences of the former ruling family in Nepal. These rented buildings have been adapted to hospital use and have served remarkably well.

But for the past three years the United Mission in Nepal has considered the possibility of building a new building for the mission hospital (called Shanta Bhawan Hospital) and all of the initial steps have now been taken to put such a plan into effect. Committees have been working on such things as getting government permission, buying land on which to build, getting customs exemption, preparing plans, determining the size of services, staff, budgets, supplies, etc.

The first general estimate is that the building will cost perhaps one million dollars. The Protestant churches of Germany have given assurances that they will provide three-fourths of the total capital costs. The United Presbyterian Church, USA, has pledged $95,000. And the cooperating missions will try in various ways to find the remaining funds that are needed ($155,000).

The United Mission, of which our World Mission Prayer League is a part, has come to believe fully in this project as an integral part of the total work of the mission in Nepal and all are praying that the Lord God will grant it. And we invite our WMPL friends and supporters to share in the partnership of prayer and faith that it may be realized.

Some projects serve all three purposes which I have mentioned. A good example of this is the Bilingual School in Cuenca, Ecuador. This school began with a kindergarten class of six or seven children a few years ago. Year by year it has grown. This year there are six grades and about 250 students.

We have struggled with the question of what more we can do to increase the usefulness of the school and have decided to go on and add a high school, with one additional class each year. We hope to be able in time to manage a school of about 500 students with twelve grades. Plans have been prepared for buying land and building a suitable school building. These plans are now in Europe where the Lutheran World Federation is considering them with the possibility of getting donations that will be enough to cover the capital costs of these building plans.

The school is a good tool for evangelism and puts the Bible into the hands of every student and into hundreds of homes in the community. All students follow good courses of Bible study in the regular curriculum of the school from the first to the last grade.

The school undoubtedly helps to strengthen the churches which are new and small and greatly overshadowed by the towering structure and the overpowering influence of Roman Catholicism in the country.

And the school meets a real need in the community. Even those who have strongly opposed an evangelical school have grudgingly admitted this. Not only have the children received a higher standard of education than they would otherwise have gotten, but they have brought to their homes a new spirit of obedience and respect for their parents, an intelligent interest in the good things of life and a concern for truth and righteousness. Many parents have expressed their sincere gratitude to the school staff for this. For them this has been a unique contribution of the school to the whole city.

These are some of the projects, the tools, we work with. There are many more. From time to time our missionary colleagues write about them in these pages. We hope that as you read about them you will help to pray for the workers and for the tools that they use, pray that God will bless them with power, grace and fruitfulness.

Perhaps you will see some way by which you can go and lend a hand in these projects. Or maybe you know someone else who can and you will want to pray that God will call them to go. Workmen are needed in every field, workmen of different kinds, with different skills. Let us not fail to pray constantly that God will call and send men and women to minister in these many places and by these many means.

# 13
# Every Christian
# a Missionary

*An article by Paul in "Lutheran World Vision," May-June 1946.*

Not long ago a theological professor declared that the great commission in Matthew 28 to "make disciples of all the nations" did not apply to the rank and file of Christians but only to the clergy and to such qualified persons as the Mission Boards of the Church might call and employ for missionary work abroad. In his opinion the ordinary Christian should not think of being a missionary, but stay at home, tend dutifully to his affairs, and support the organized program of the Church.

This was not the opinion of the Early Church. After Pentecost the Church spread abroad rapidly, powerfully, effectively. All believers were missionaries. The whole Church was a missionary society. Nay, more —it was an army of revolutionists. Wherever they went, they produced upheavals, revivals, revolutions. They were full of moral dynamite. The fire of God burned in them. They set out to change men's lives. They aimed to turn the world upside down. There was a freshness about them, a fearlessness, a reckless abandon, a hilarious faith, and a tender love which enabled them to overleap the most difficult barriers, suffer unspeakable hardships, and win their enemies to Christ.

Their weapons appeared weak and harmless, but proved to

be "mighty before God to the pulling down of strongholds." They used only the Word of God, fervent prayer, the testimony of faith, and the fire of the Holy Spirit. Their methods were strange, unnatural, and radical. They loved their enemies and prayed for them. They preached "Christ and him crucified" without fear. They sacrificed beyond measure for the gospel and "loved not their lives even unto death."

The spontaneous, overflowing expansion of the Early Church was not dependent upon material wealth but on the power of the Holy Spirit, and was always connected with poverty and sacrifice. Everyone who had received life by faith from Christ felt inwardly constrained to preach and spread the gospel. In this there was no great distinction between clergy and laity. All the saints were priests, ambassadors, and stewards of the mystery of God's grace. There existed no professional class of "home" or "foreign" missionaries. Every believer, however weak, poor or unlearned was "called," "commissioned," "sent."

Some changes have come in the missionary methods of the Church since those early times. There has come the formation of a separate missionary class, grouped in missionary societies, supported by special mission funds, working through mission stations and missionary institutions. These methods have achieved great and glorious results in all parts of the world. Yet these accomplishments have cost dearly if they have had the effect of making the vast bulk of Christians content and satisfied to be non-missionaries and of dimming in them the vision to be wholly devoted first and last, in every circumstance, to Christ's program of worldwide evangelization. Many may be led to feel that because they do not measure up to the high qualifications of a professional missionary that they therefore bear no great responsibility to the heathen. Or some may feel that because they support some mission they are thereby reaching the heathen by proxy. Some actually suppose that by hiring a pastor for their church, they are thus, through him, fulfilling their mission towards the unconverted.

We believe, however, that there are hundreds and hundreds of lay people throughout the Church who feel their calling as the early Christians did, and in whose hearts there burns the desire to spread the gospel in the regions beyond. Their life and testimony could greatly assist and supplement the program of Christian missions. Perhaps many have been held up because they saw no opportunity of any kind for them in foreign fields. Perhaps others have not been able to find a way by which they could go.

We believe that the mission fields are bristling with opportunities. We also believe that there are numerous ways by which multitudes of fearless and devoted followers of Christ can go into all parts of the world and put in their hands to help reap the whitened harvest of our generation. If you long to go but don't know what you can do, or how you can go, we invite you to write to us. It may be that we can suggest a course which would be helpful to you. We are dedicated to the one business of praying and working to get laborers into the harvest field and we shall be happy to help in any way we can those who wish to give their lives for evangelizing the world.

# 14
# Living by Faith

*A tract message printed by Lutheran Colportage Service in the early years of the Mission.*

The Christian life is begun by faith, and it is the plan and purpose of God that this life should be maintained, developed and exploited by faith.   There are quite a few who have learned to know by experience that helpless and hopeless sinners may be justified before God by faith in Jesus as their Savior. But ever so many have stopped there and have failed to discover the further truth that those who are justified by faith are to live their whole lives in all details by faith.  The "law of faith" (Romans 3:27) is to be the foundation principle and the governing law of their entire life in all its phases.

The basis for this truth is clearly presented in the New Testament:

**First**:  All life is in Jesus.  In him "are all the treasures of wisdom and knowledge hidden." "For all things were created by him and through him and unto him . . . and by him all things consist." And today as ever, "He upholds all things by the word of his power." "For it was the Father's good pleasure that **in him should all fullness dwell.**"

"All in all forever, Jesus will I sing.
Everything in Jesus, and Jesus everything."

Thus "in him was the life..." and in him is fullness of wisdom, righteousness, holiness, power, redemption, health, riches and authority, etc.

**Second:** This wonderful Jesus in all his fullness is God's precious gift to his church "... which is his body, and fullness of him that filleth all in all." He is alive forevermore to live in his saints, to be their life, and to both will and do the powerful purposes of God in and through them. "When Christ who is our life shall be manifested ..." "I have been crucified with Christ, and it is no longer I that live, but Christ liveth in me." "... that the life also of Jesus might be manifested in our mortal bodies." "In him ye are made full (or complete)."

All resources, all wealth, all strength and health, all power and authority, all forgiveness and redemption, all the fullness of God—all this is the possession of the believer. In fact, **"all things are yours."** And all this is contained **within** the believer as Christ dwells in him. He is the temple of the Holy Spirit and the glory of the Lord may fill him as it once filled the temple of God of old. He is the earthen vessel which holds "the exceeding greatness of the power of God" (2 Cor. 4:7).

But more: all these riches of the life of God in us are immediately and constantly available to the believer. He can exercise and wield the power and authority of God. He can dispense health and wealth just as Peter said to the crippled man, "What I have that I give thee; in the name of Jesus Christ stand up and walk." He can employ "the power which worketh in us" to effectively move mountains, overcome adversaries, and reign as a triumphant conqueror in any and every circumstance. He can, in short, "manifest the life of Jesus in his body" (2 Cor. 4:10-11).

**Third:** How can this be? How is it done? The answer is simple: by FAITH. "As therefore ye received Christ Jesus the Lord (How? By faith!) so walk in him" (Colossians 2:6). The grace of God and his fullness are given without measure and are poured out in a constant and continuous supply. Faith believes this and draws upon it, takes it, appropriates it, and opens the door for its free activity. There is Christ, my fullness, and here am I with my need. Faith links the two—brings them together.

1. By faith we have access to the grace of God. Romans 5:2
2. By faith we are the children of God. Galations 3:26
3. By faith we have the righteousness of God. Philippians 3:9
4. By faith we have forgiveness and sanctification. Acts 26:18
5. By faith we are cleansed. Acts. 15:9
6. By faith Christ dwells in us. Ephesians 3:17
7. By faith we inherit God's promises. Hebrews 8:12
8. By faith we have victory over the world. 1 John 5:4
9. By faith we are triumphant over difficulties. Heb. 11:33-40
10. By faith we can overcome the evil one. Ephesians 6:16

The Bible gives the record of men who, when they were commissioned by God to some certain task, obeyed and took by faith everything needful to accomplish what they were called to do. Thus, "By faith Moses" kept the passover, crossed the Red Sea, brought forth water from the rock and bread from heaven, and led and guided a great nation for forty years in a desert. Thus, "By faith Abraham, when he was called, obeyed to go out to a place which he was to receive as an inheritance." Thus, Joshua conquered a land full of giants. Thus, Gideon sent home 29,700 men of his army and with only three hundred left, he stood by faith and watched the terror of the Lord confuse and destroy his enemies. Thus, by faith men "obtained promises, stopped the mouths of lions, quenched the power of fire, from weakness were made strong," etc. The power of God was present all the time, ready for action. Faith saw it, believed it, took it, released it, and saw it work.

It is thus that a Christian is to live by faith—live the life of God, let Jesus live in him, and do the mighty works of God which "God has before prepared that we should walk in them." By an act of faith you may receive him and his fullness. By a constant succession of acts of faith the outflow of his fullness may become your habitual experience. This is not done once and for all, but is a continuous taking of a continuous supply from Jesus himself as he dwells with us. It is a moment-by-moment faith and dependence on Jesus who dwells moment-by-moment in our hearts, ready ever to give all that we can take. As you trust him, he will supply all your need. The moment you begin to believe is the moment you begin to receive, and as long as you keep believing you will be sure to receive. He wants our faith to be as constant as his supply.

What are your needs today in the calling of life service for which God in his grace has made you personally responsible? The supply is in Jesus, and if you are a Christian, he lives in you to supply all your needs according to his riches in glory. Do you need patience, strength to do his will, love, health, or courage? It is all in Christ. Take him. Take what you need from him. It is all within you for he who is king of all is within you. Take it on the authority of the Word of God. Receive it, thank him for what you have received, and go forth in obedience, acting upon the full possession of it.

# 15
# Three Questions

*Excerpt from a letter by Paul Lindell in reply to a letter from a WMPL missionary, March 22, 1951.*

Dear ____,

The questions which you ask are very searching questions and very good ones. They touch the very root of our walk with God and the main point of our service together for the Lord.

1—**"Should I be willing to go anywhere?"** I believe the answer should be YES. You have put this question as number one, and that is where it should be because it is very fundamental. If we are not clear on this question then the others will not find a very clear answer either.

We must be willing for anything because we are not our own but are the servants of Christ. A master knows what he wants done and he also knows which of his servants he wants to do each job. You remember how Moses sincerely doubted God's judgment in assigning him to lead Israel out of Egypt and had an argument with God about it. And Gideon did the same thing. Sarah thought God was very foolish to make her, an old woman, the mother of a chosen nation. The sainted old prophet Samuel wondered very much why God passed up the noble, strong sons of Jesse when he wanted a king for the people and why he had to select a small shepherd boy for this great job. But it was because David had a willing spirit. It was later said of him by God that David was a "man after my own heart," for he did what God assigned to him. David himself saw the value of this spirit and in Psalm fifty-one after confessing his sin he cried to God to "uphold me with a willing spirit; then will I teach transgressors thy ways and sinners shall be converted to thee."

Unless we have a willing spirit it will be very hard for God to guide us. But if we are free in heart and keep a simple trust in the Lord that he will keep us in his way, then he can move us around just as he pleases. Sometimes to get us going in the right direction he must turn us first one way and then another, just as a pilot turns the rudder of the ship this way and that way to get the ship on the course. What a job he would have if the rudder got stuck and did not move freely.

I met a rather homely-looking Hawaiian girl working in a furniture factory in New York. I have been there and preached in that factory several times and have met this girl and she has sung at the meetings. Her voice is not sweet, her looks are not good, and she is not gifted. But when she stood up with piles of lumber all around and stacks of half-finished furniture and sang "I would love to tell you what I think of Jesus," the men stopped talking as they sat around eating their noon lunch and then I had a chance to preach to them. Her spirit was full of love. They dumped their troubles on her, not because she could do anything about them but because she seemed to have a love big enough to listen and to care. And yet she told me with tears that she wished she was good enough to be missionary! Why, she was the Lord's ministering angel to scores of men and women in a hard-boiled factory where no fancy missionary could ever go and work. The Lord knows his business. He has good reasons for putting us where we are, and if we just spill love everywhere he will by it cover a multitude of sins and help lots of people.

**2—"Is it right to go any place without inner peace—just because others want you to go, or because there is a need?"**

Does the need make the call?

It is hard to answer these questions with only a few words. I have discovered that missionaries have more trouble with this matter of "inner peace" than almost anything else. And I sometimes feel that it is because they have some rather wrong ideas about it.

The reason for an individual's not having peace about something is often very hard to find, and the reason for not having peace in a group decision is still harder to find.

Sometimes people do not have "peace" about something at conference meetings because they are not absolutely open and do not freely share their opinions on matters as they come up. Then behind the scenes they talk with only certain choice friends and stir up dissensions.

Some are afraid to face the facts and so cannot get peace on certain matters. Others are afraid to venture ahead and for lack of faith they lack peace.

A tendency to indecision is poor soil for peace. The person who takes a long time to decide things, and then after they are decided, undecides them for fear of making a mistake, will always have trouble with having no peace. The fear of making a mistake makes him make a continuous mistake, the mistake of being always emotionally upset due to indecision. Far better to make a few wrong decisions than to be indecisive. For an indecisive person is in far greater danger of making wrong decisions. And he will rarely have peace for very long about anything.

In Mexico I called on aged Dr. Dale who had been in Mexico for fifty years and is the leader of the Mexican Indian Mission. I asked him what had been his greatest trouble through the years in the work, and he told me that his greatest trouble had been with missionaries whose consciences were too sensitive and who could not adjust their minds to working by the ways which the situation required. They slowed up the program of the mission.

It was a great revelation in my life when I saw that God will guide a man's life by the decisions of a group. If I am called to work with a group, such as our mission, then I believe that God will guide me very often by the decisions of the group. And if the decision has been a mistake it will soon be apparent to all and the group will change the decision to fit the case. It is a great thing to learn to trust God in the group. If a person really learns to do this he will walk with peace. If I were to have my own way I would go to the mission field with my family, but the council has assigned me to the work here at home. And because first of all I am committed to the Mission, and because I believe that God guides those who are responsible in this fellowship, and because when in conference with them the best opinion is that I should stay at home, I therefore take this as the Lord's direction and it gives me peace. And by going ahead as best I can with the assignment given me, the Lord has sustained me with his blessed peace.

3—**"Is God not interested in the individual? Or will anybody do for any job?"** Yes indeed God is very interested in the individual. Remember, not a hair falls to the ground without his loving knowledge and attention.

Most often there are more jobs to be done than there are people to do them. Jesus meant this when he said that the harvest was plentiful and the workers were few. And so many of us have to try to do many things which we think we cannot do.

Another thing is this: When you join a mission like ours it is like joining a family. There are many things which have to be done in family life and sometimes it is well to take turns at doing them. We do this at our home here in Minneapolis. We take turns at dishes, washing floors, repair work, firing the furnace, shovelling snow, and many other things, including taking charge of meetings and carrying on the administrative tasks. Some can do some things better than others. But we take it on as a family and all pitch in as best we can because the work must be done. And so we try to make the adjustments which will work out best.

The place isn't the most important thing. A person at rest with God and full of love can make any place into a little heaven where hungry souls can find Jesus. "While place we seek, or place we shun, the soul finds happiness in none; But with my God to guide my way, 'tis equal joy to go or stay.'" This is what a woman wrote in prison after she had lost all her wealth and had been scarred by small pox and then had been thrown in prison by French priests because of her evangelical faith. And she made the prison shine with God's glory.

Now I must close. "May the Lord of peace himself give you peace at all times and in all ways" (2 Thess. 3:16).

# 16

# The Apostle Paul's Fourfold Example

As we look at the Apostle Paul we see in him the leading example, outside of the life and ministry of Jesus himself, of what it is like to be a missionary and how to go about answering God's call to make the gospel known wherever he sends us.

I would like to take a scene from the life of the apostle and from it learn four things, four things one might expect as we go forth as missionaries of the gospel. We read from the last chapter of the book of Acts, reading a few verses here and there, beginning with verse 11.

"After three months we set sail in a ship which had wintered in the island, a ship of Alexandria with the Twin Brothers as figurehead. Putting in at Syracuse we stayed there for three days. And from there we made a circuit and arrived at Rheium and after one day a south wind sprang up and on the second day we came to Puteoli. There we found brethren and we were invited to say with them for seven days. And so we came to Rome. And the brethren there, when they heard of us, came as far as the Forum of Appius, and the Three Taverns to meet us. On seeing them Paul thanked God and took courage. And when we came into Rome, Paul was allowed to stay by himself, with a soldier that guarded him."

You may remember that Paul was captured in Jerusalem by his enemies. They raised a great riot in the temple courtyard and then it spilled out into the street. They tried to break him down and beat him to death but he was rescued by the Roman guard of the temple. He was hurried into the castle. Later he was moved from Jerusalem to Caesarea for his safe keeping. And there he was kept for two years in prison. While there he appealed his case to be heard by the emperor of Rome as was his right as a Roman citizen. He was the object of the hatred of Jews who had despised Jesus and the message about Jesus as the Messiah. They were determined to kill him and to get him out of the way, and to destroy the Church, just as Paul himself before his conversion had been determined to wipe out the Church and the followers of Jesus Christ.

Now then all winter long he had been on his way from Caesarea to Rome. Along the way they experienced shipwrecks and had to winter on an island. Finally he had come to Rome and was chained to a Roman soldier and allowed to stay in a house, a rented house, instead of being put in prison, until his case could be heard by the emperor.

While he was in the house he called together the leaders of the Jews and talked to them about the gospel of Jesus, saying, "For this reason therefore, I have asked to see you and speak with you, since it is because of the hope of Israel that I am bound with this chain" (Acts 28:20). Then in verse 23 we read, "When they had appointed a day for him, they came to him at his lodging in great numbers. And he expounded the matter to them from morning till evening, testifying to the Kingdom of God and trying to convince them about Jesus both from the law of Moses and from the prophets. And some were convinced by what he said, while others disbelieved. So, as they disagreed among themselves, they departed after Paul had made one statement: "The Holy Spirit was right in saying to your fathers through Isaiah the prophet. . ." Paul then quoted from Isaiah and said to them, "Let it be known to you then that this salvation of God has been sent to the Gentiles; they will listen."

"And he lived there two whole years at his own expense, and welcomed all who came to him, preaching the kingdom of God and teaching about the Lord Jesus Christ quite openly and unhindered."

It is hard to understand how God's chief missionary could be tied up for so long as a prisoner. Some Bible scholars think that Saint Paul spent half of his missionary career in jail, in confinement, hounded there by his enemies. Before he even began his public ministry as a missionary he had been restrained. From the days of his conversion he knew that God had called him to preach the gospel, but for nearly ten years he was restrained from doing anything about it.

For ten years Paul did nothing as a missionary until he came down to Antioch, brought there by Barnabas, and then after a year and a half of fellowship in the church at Antioch, he began his missionary journeys. Paul is a man who had a most unusual call from God, and yet one big factor about his life is that his ministry was under constant restrictions. He is restrained here and he is restricted there.

I think through the years of our gospel ministry we will find there are reins that hold us, circumstances that will restrain us. We will constantly be straining at the limitations. Do not think this strange. It comes in the course of being sent by Jesus into the world that is hostile toward God. Our Lord Jesus himself found it that way. His ministry was limited in time—barely three and one-half years.

Throughout the world this is true of the missionary movement. It labors constantly under limitations. There are limitations of personnel. Nearly every mission I know about anywhere in the world is limited by the number of people. They all need more missionaries. They are all limited in their staffs and in the number of workers that they need to do the job well. There are hospitals and schools and missionary institutions of all kinds working all the time with half the needed staff. Limited by the shortage of workers. Jesus said it would be that way. "The harvest is plentiful, but the laborers are few." They were few in Jesus' day. They have been few ever since. They are few today.

Now we may not think that is so. There are about 40,000 missionaries from North America working across the world in a hundred different countries today. But when you start to spread out amongst those hundred countries, all that there is to do, the distribution gets pretty thin. There are limitations in the number of workers. There are limitations in supply, in equipment, in what there is to work with. There are limitations of money. There are limitations of time and strength. Ah, there are many, many limitations that bind and hold one, as Saint Paul was held by a chain to a Roman soldier. He was on a leash and confined to a house, and always had this iron chain rattling on his arm, fastened to a soldier. That was as far as he could go. And still here he was God's ambassador to the nations and trying to do his job under limitations.

There is, however, a note of cheer here. We see that Saint Paul lived in the house in Rome and welcomed all who came to him, preaching and teaching about the Lord Jesus quite openly. Within limitations there is a freedom of spirit and of opportunity given by God so that preaching and teaching about Jesus Christ can go on openly and unhindered. You might put a chain on Paul's arm but no one can put a chain on his spirit, his heart, his mind or his faith. Limitations need not get us down. Jesus' promise still holds good, "... that from within there shall flow forth rivers of living water. This he spake of the Holy Spirit which they that believed on him were to receive." Since the day of Pentecost, the Holy Spirit has come to fill the lives of his people. And that can be unlimited and without hindrance.

So, in the second place, I would like to assure you that God has fullness of life and spirit in Christ available by the Holy Spirit so that we can welcome all who come within the limits of our circumstances and there we can minister the truth about Jesus Christ openly and unhindered.

There is a third thing to note about Saint Paul. The Jewish leaders gathered at the house where he was confined and heard his message. They listened to his preaching, but not all of them believed. Some believed, some doubted, and some went away wagging their heads. But Paul reminds them of what the Holy Spirit said by the prophet Isaiah: "Go to this people, and say, 'You shall indeed hear but never understand, and you shall indeed see but never perceive. For this people's heart has grown dull, and their ears are heavy of hearing.'"

As Paul saw them walk away without heeding the message, he adds, "Let it be known to you then that this salvation of God has been sent to the Gentiles; they will listen." Notice those three words, "They will listen." The people that the

Jews called "dogs" will listen, says Paul. When the gospel about Jesus comes to them they will listen. That seems to me to be one of the most magnificent statements of faith in the New Testament. It shows the attitude of Saint Paul. He has an absolute trust in his message, the gospel, for "it is the power of God to salvation to everyone who believes." He has an absolute trust in the Holy Spirit, that the Holy Spirit will take the word which he preaches about Jesus and will find a way to get it into the hearts of unbelievers, of Gentiles, of outsiders. God has a way to open the eyes of people so they see the truth of Jesus, and to open their minds to receive and understand it, and to open their hearts to long for and to believe it, and to repent of their sins and to turn in faith and find salvation in him.

I am glad to say that throughout the world and the missionary movement there is a vast amount of that kind of faith. If it were not so there would be little progress. There are many who say every day they get up and go to work, "They will listen." The people will listen. Children will listen. Mothers and fathers will listen. College students will listen. Government officials will listen. They will listen. Where there is no faith, where there is no knowledge of Christ, where there has been opposition to the gospel, ah, there will be those who will listen. Day by day men and women, in strong confidence, labor faithfully with the good news in simple, expectant faith.

One of the pioneer missionaries in Africa was a doctor. He was the father-in-law to David Livingston. Some friends in England wrote to him saying they would like to send him a special gift—"something you don't have but would love to have, something extra. Only tell us, we'll send it to you." The old missionary thought it over along with his wife. They wrote home to England saying, "Yes, there is something we'd like to have that we don't have. We would be greatly pleased if you could send it to us. Send us a little communion set for the celebreation of the Lord's Supper. Oh, we don't have any church here, just me and my wife. We don't have a single brother in the faith. There isn't a single believer, not yet, but there will be. They will believe. The day will come. We'd like to be ready for it so when there are people who gather around the Lord's table we can be ready with a decent cup and plate to celebrate the supper of our Lord." The friends in England sent them a cup and plate. How long did they wait for the first believer to join them? Sixteen years. Then came the first one to share the wine and the bread with them.

There was a Lutheran missionary named Gunderson who went to Africa. He had been a young clerk in a bank in Iowa. One morning as he was cleaning up the office before business, he came across a tract and by it God called him to Africa. Before he left he had some additonal schooling. As some of his friends gathered to see him off, they formed a little Lutheran mission that used to be called the Gunderson Mission, which in time became known as the Lutheran Sudan Mission.

In the city where Gunderson and his wife began their work they were looked on as intruding foreigners. The leading citizens were particularly set against them, with the result that nobody came in the door when they held their meetings. The Gundersons had a little pump organ. While his wife played the organ, Gunderson and his children sat on the front bench as they held their regular services. They threw open the windows so anybody in the street could hear and though they made their witness as loud as they could, nobody came in.

How long would you keep that up? A month, six months? Wouldn't you take a look at the situation after a while and say, "What's the use? We do not get anybody in. We keep preaching but not producing any fruit. We had better close the place down." They didn't close the place down. They kept right at it. For how long? For nine years. After nine years one of the leading men in town faced a crisis in his life. He sent for Gunderson and asked him to come and pray for him. He went and prayed for him and God answered his prayer. And it turned the tide. The needy family came to the little chapel and soon it was filled with people. They soon had to find other places to meet that could accommodate more people. It changed the attitude of the entire city. They will listen, he said. For nine years he said that, and he preached to his family as the kids grew up, and preached loud enough so that anybody passing in the street could hear. They will listen, he said. And they did, after nine years.

One last thought. Notice what Saint Luke, the writer, says

in verse thirty: "And he (Paul) lived there two whole years at his own expense, and welcomed all who came to him." Why would he throw in that "he lived at his own expense"? He could have had free room and board over in the jail. But they gave him the option to rent a house and to board himself, while he waited for his trial to come up. He waited two years, paying his own rent and keep. Why? Because it was more comfortable? I am sure that was not the real reason. It was because he took advantage of the opportunity that it gave him to reach a wider audience than he could from the jail. And so he paid the rent out of his own pocket.

Now this reveals something about the Apostle Paul, his attitude, his spirit. He had a giving spirit. He was in the business of giving, not getting. What he had in his pockets he regarded as being available for the cause of the gospel. So he made it reach as far as possible.

I work in a fellowship, the World Mission Prayer League, in which there are many of our people who do their work, and sometimes rent their houses, at their own expense and are constantly paying out of their own pockets for this, that and the other thing in their work in order to get something done that otherwise would not get done. We see that happening amongst us all the time. And that is a healthy sign. There will be fruitfulness in the missionary movement as long as there is that kind of a giving spirit. But when the springs of giving and springs of out-pouring dry up then there will be a drought, a famine. Things will dry up.

As we catch these glimpses of the Apostle Paul and his spirit, may God bless us and build us up and enable us to fulfill our calling, to run the course with joy and complete it in the power of the Holy Spirit.

# 17
# The Any-Century Missionary

*Part of a message by Paul given at the Sixth International Student Missionary Convention, Urbana, Illinois, 1962. Used by permission of Inter-Varsity Press.*

What kind of people does it take to do this work in the world today, to answer God's call, to be sent by God's Spirit, and to be commissioned by his Church? What kind of people are required to share in bringing the gospel to our generation in all parts of the world?

In answering this question, mission boards and societies have sometimes listed various qualifications for various kinds of work. But when we talk about the kind of people required by God, we need first to go back twenty centuries to the Early Church, to that group of disciples who first followed Christ. There we shall discover the kind of men and women God wants to use, the sort of person God sends—then and now. Through such people he will bear fruit in all places, on all assignments, and under all conditions throughout the world. They are his servants and ambassadors, who preach in Christ's name the good news of the gospel, showing the fruits of his love in their lives.

I'd like to read most of a familiar passage in Paul's second letter to the Corinthians, chapter 4:1-12 and verses 16-18.

Therefore, being engaged in this service (or, having this ministry) by the mercy of God, we do not lose heart. We have renounced disgraceful, underhanded ways; we refuse to practice cunning or to tamper with God's Word, but by the open statement of the truth we would commend ourselves to every man's conscience in the sight of God. And even if our gospel is veiled, it is veiled only to those who are perishing. In their case the god of this world has blinded the minds of the unbelievers, to keep them from seeing the light of the gospel of the glory of Christ, who is the likeness of God. For what we preach is not ourselves, but Jesus Christ as Lord, with ourselves as your servants for Jesus' sake. For it is the God who said, 'Let light shine out of darkness,' who has shone in our hearts to give the light of the knowledge of the glory of God in the face of Christ.

But we have this treasure in earthen vessels, to show that the transcendent power belongs to God and not to us. We are afflicted in every way, but not crushed; perplexed, but not driven to despair; persecuted, but not forsaken; struck down, but not destroyed; always carrying in the body the death of Jesus, so that the life of Jesus may also be manifested in our bodies. For while we live we are always being given up to death for Jesus' sake, so that the life of Jesus may be manifested in our mortal flesh. So death is at work in us, but life in you. . . .

So we do not lose heart. Though our outer nature is wasting away, our inner nature is being renewed every day. For this slight momentary affliction is preparing for us an eternal weight of glory beyond all comparison, because we look not to the things that are seen but to the things that are unseen; for the things that are seen are transient, but the things that are unseen are eternal.

From these verses and a few elsewhere in the New Testament, I'd like to single out three things that should distinguish a missionary in this or any generation.

## BEARING THIS TREASURE

In verse seven the apostle says, "We have this treasure in earthen vessels, to show that the transcendent power belongs to God and not to us." What distinguishes a missionary of Jesus Christ is that he comes bearing a treasure. This marks him as different from all other men. A child of God is one who has a treasure. "We **have** this treasure," says the Apostle Paul. We've got it. We're not on a long search for some hidden, mysterious treasure way off in the distance. We come bearing to the world a treasure we possess. We have it in our hands. We've seen it with our eyes. We've felt it. We've tasted it. We possess it.

That is the certain triumphant note which the New Testament sounds; that is the note this world needs today. There are many people who are forever seeking for truth they never find. They say, "I think that's the way. I think you'll find truth in this or that direction." Or they say, "There are many ways. Any way will do." In our generation a voice that needs to be heard is that of the man or woman who says, "I have this truth. I have found this treasure. Here it is. Let me tell you about it."

"We have this treasure," said the apostle. And in his ministry in his day, he circled the Roman Empire, bringing to people the good news of that treasure—which he possessed, which was in his heart, which was his life.

There are many things in God's Word that are exceedingly precious to the Christian. Of these, I single out four mighty treasures that we must know and have in this day.

1—**The Treasure of Christ.** First, when the apostle says, "We have this treasure," he has just been speaking of Jesus Christ in this way: "In their case," he says, "the god of this world has blinded the minds of the unbelievers, to keep them from seeing the light of the gospel of the glory of Christ, who is the likeness of God. For what we preach is not ourselves, but Jesus Christ as Lord, with ourselves as your servants for Jesus' sake. For it is the God who said, 'Let light shine out of darkness,' who has shone in our hearts to give the light of the knowledge of the glory of God in the face of Christ."

"He is the treasure," says the apostle. First and foremost, the treasure we have and bear to this world is Jesus Christ. We come to speak of Jesus Christ to our generation, to tell men plainly and simply about Jesus—not to argue about him, not to debate about him, not to have speculative discussions about him, but to bear witness to him. When you read the Book of Acts, there is something so simple, so gripping, so moving, so winsome about the way in which the Early Church spoke of Jesus Christ.

What do his early followers say about him? In the Book of Acts, in the Letters of the Apostle Paul, and on throughout the New Testament, one thing they always said about Jesus Christ is, "He is alive." Whenever they spoke of him, they stressed this fact: "He's alive; He's risen from the dead." He died outside Jerusalem on a hill. Many people saw him die, people who had heard him preach and seen the miracles he had done. Then on that sad day they saw him lifted up on a cross, and he was put to death. He was taken down and buried in a tomb, and they thought the story was finished. But on Easter Sunday morning, he rose from the grave. "He's alive! We've seen him, we've talked with him, we know he's alive."

Second, they said about him, "He's here. He's here with us. We live and walk in his presence. He's not gone off, removing himself from us. He's here." In simple words, with joy, they spoke of their conviction, and they lived in the strength of that conviction.

What convinced them of his presence? Their conviction was rooted primarily in his word. "He said he'd be with us. He told us he'd go away and come again. He promised that he would be with us even to the end of the age. 'I'll be with you,' he said. He made that promise." Will he keep it? "Oh, yes. He promised that he would rise from the dead, and he did. He promised that he will be with us, and he is. We know by his promise." They knew by faith, and God bore witness to their faith, and they experienced anew his promise.

When the Holy Spirit did come upon these early followers, they were all filled by him, and they walked and lived in his presence. Yet there was something familiar in this new experience, for the Holy Spirit was the Spirit of Christ. He was their Savior. He was their Master. They knew him. God simply had come to live with them in a new way, and Christ was present with them from that day on.

Third, they said, "He is Lord; He is the Lord God." Wherever they went, they proclaimed Jesus Christ as Lord. "We preach the Lord Jesus Christ to you. We preach unto you Jesus as Lord. He is God." They worshiped him, they submitted to him, they lived under his rule as God and Lord of their lives.

Fourth, they said, "He gives forgiveness to sinners." They went on to speak about how he had lived and how he had died, and what the Old Testament Scriptures had to say about his death, and how the Holy Spirit gave them an understanding of the significance of his death. And they proclaimed to all the world that through Jesus Christ and his death and resurrection there is forgiveness of sins for undeserving sinners.

Fifth, they declared this gospel of forgiveness to be absolutely free to anybody, anywhere—the vilest, most hopeless sinner was offered in Jesus Christ forgiveness from God, the Holy God.

This was their treasure. Wherever they went, they spoke of this treasure of Jesus Christ

**2—The Treasure of the Church.** A second treasure set forth in the New Testament is that of the Church. The New Testament, from the Book of Acts on, is the story of the Church. The Epistles are letters written to churches. The Book of Acts tells how the Church was born, and how the Lord added to its number day by day; how local churches were formed and how they developed; how the life of God was lived corporately and how this life bore fruit in various churches, in congregations.

Wherever men came to believe in Jesus Christ, they somehow moved together. They were always found in clusters—not as single pilgrims marching in separate directions. You find them still in bunches. Some people say, "Well of course, in those days they got together for their mutual protection, because society was against them and they were afraid that others would treat them as they had treated their Savior." But this isn't how the Church spoke of it. When they came to express their understanding of this wonderful coming together of fellow believers, of fellow Christians, they had something much more wonderful to say about it than that. They said, "We are the family of God. In this family we find people who have received a birth from above, a birth of the life of God in their hearts. By faith in Jesus Christ we have been born into his family, adopted as sons and daughters. Thus we find ourselves brothers and sisters in the family of God. In this family, all distinctions that have existed to separate us from one another are gone. There is neither male nor female, there is neither rich nor poor, there is neither slave nor free, there is neither Jew nor Gentile; we are all one in Jesus Christ. We have a new citizenship now, in heaven. And here on earth, life in God has broken the bonds of nationalism, crossing also other lines of social, and economic, and cultural distinction, so that we've all been drawn together in the one wonderful family of God."

This oneness was a reality, and the realization of it brought them together. They weren't just dreaming dreams. They found this unity to be true, and they lived in the reality of their experience. It was a precious thing to them, but it was more than that. They came to speak of this fellowship as the body of Christ. The Apostle Paul spoke of how this mystery had been hidden for ages, but was now made known. For us the mystery stands unveiled; we've been allowed to enter into it, and here now together we are joined as part of the Body of Christ, of which he is the head. In this body we are not only members of Christ, but we are members one of another. There is a thrilling interdependence in this body, for the Holy Spirit has given to its members many varieties of gifts, all of which are needful for the building up and nourishment of the body, so that one part cannot function apart from another. Here in this body, Christ is present, for he said that where two or three even are gathered together in his name, he is there in the midst of them.

This knowledge was a joy to the early disciples; it was a delight to them. In this body, in this life together, Christ dwelt and worked unfolding his plans and purposes for the world. They valued the fellowship of believers, they loved the coming together of God's people, and they did not even consider living their Christian life apart from the Church.

3—**The Treasure of the Word.** Third, as you read the New Testament, wherever you find the Church meeting together and doing its work effectively, you find it centered on the Word of God. The early disciples immediately turned their attention to the Old Testament Scriptures. They related these Scriptures to what was happening around them, and they believed that the Holy Spirit was speaking out of Moses, the Psalms, and the Prophets to their present situation. They recalled the words of Jesus, his life and ministry. In time, some of them wrote down their recollections, but to begin with, they shared the spoken words, and later the letters that were passed among the churches. All these, they treasured. Then men stood up in congregations and preached. In all this, men waited for God to speak. They waited for the Word of God. The life of the Church rested on the Word of God. The conversion of people was dependent on preaching, expounding, and holding forth the Word of God—for God worked through his Word.

In later years people came to speak of the written Word of God as a means of grace, for God brings his grace of salvation to men through his Word. Christ comes to men through his Word. Later Peter writes in his second letter, "His divine power has granted to us all things that pertain to life and godliness, through the knowledge of him who called us to his own glory and excellence, by which he has granted to us his precious and very great promises, that through these you may escape from the corruption that is in the world because of passion and become partakers of the divine nature" (RSV). So a part of this precious treasure which they had in their hands and worked with was the written Word of God.

4—**The Treasure of Their Calling.** A fourth treasure was the ministry which the disciples were given by their Lord. They had a calling. They had a job to do. They had a vocation. They were not just turned loose and sent to drift somehow through life, finding their own way. God had a task for them, an appointment, a way to live and a way to serve, an object and an end in view that they were to accomplish, thus fulfilling his will. I don't see much difference in the nature of this treasure for the early disciples and for us today. The treasure is the same.

Two things impress me as I think of the New Testament teaching on this matter. First, these Christian people clearly held the idea that their daily employment was the will of God—God's plan and purpose for them; that when they labored, they were laboring not for man, but for Christ. They were servants of Jesus, not merely while they were preaching the gospel or working in a church gathering, but while they were working at the carpenter's bench, seated on the judge's bench, or about the business of buying and selling. Whatever their daily task was, they were to do all they did in the name and for the glory of Jesus Christ. They were to serve not men, but God.

What a radical idea that was! How it transformed their whole outlook on life! And what a transformation that would make in our day and generation, when men are serving primarily themselves, if you and I did our work as before the Lord—at his command, in his presence, and for his sake.

The time to start working with that approach is right now in school. I know that's rather a radical idea to apply in your biology lab, for example, or to the next term paper. When I went to college, it was during the depression. I'd just come from China, so this country was quite new to me, and I didn't know what depressions were or what this one would mean for me. I was lucky to get a job at all. My job that helped me through college was cleaning out men's washrooms in a large dormitory. I had come to real personal faith and experience of the grace of God not long before that, during revival days in central China when I was a high-school senior. Now in that dormitory job, I wondered how in the world to relate my daily work to being a servant of Jesus Christ.

What does this have to do with being a missionary? It's got everything to do with being a missionary. There are many tasks. There is traffic to direct, there are gas stations to run, there are legislatures where laws must be passed and taxes collected, there is research to do, there are diseases to cure, there are thousands of things to do that relate to our daily, normal, natural life. God means that his people shall plunge into these tasks as his servants.

The New Testament people had that idea. They looked at the task God put before them and said, "It's a privilege to walk through life, carrying on my daily work, not for myself or my boss only, but for Jesus Christ whom I serve."

Second, in their ministry the disciples were to be servants to others. They were called to minister to people. The Apostle Paul says that very plainly: "For what we preach is not ourselves, but Jesus Christ as Lord, with ourselves as your servants for Jesus' sake." Christ called his disciples to be servants. He himself came as a servant. "I came not to be ministered unto, but to minister"—to be a servant, to be a slave to you. Part of the amazing ministry to which we're called in our day is to be servants. There'll always be a place of service for you in the worldwide Church of Jesus Christ as long as you'll be a servant.

The disciples were called also to be ambassadors, to bring with them wherever they went the message of reconciliation. They were given the authority to go to men and say, "God will forgive your sins through Jesus Christ. I come in his name. I am authorized to plead with you to be reconciled through Jesus Christ to God." The ministry of being a servant and an ambassador of Christ is part of the wonderful treasure we have.

The Apostle Paul says, "We have this treasure. We **have** this treasure." It's been given to us. Our day needs men and women who also can say, "We have this treasure. We come with this treasure."

## IN EARTHEN VESSELS

Paul further says, "We have this treasure in earthen vessels." What a picture that is! Some day some of you may ride in an Indian train across North India and stop at one of the stations where you may get a drink of milk. It will be served to you in a little clay cup. When you're through with it, you can toss the cup, dash it to pieces, off the platform preferably. The milk is given to you in a clay vessel. Many parts of the world understand the service of a clay vessel. It's weak, faulty, not much to look at, and easily disposed of. We have this treasure, says the Apostle, in earthen vessels.

Sometimes missionaries get to feel (I have myself), "God, why give your treasure to earthen vessels? Why haven't you given this ministry to the angels? Angels don't need passports, they don't have to get visas, they don't have to ride on ships or airplanes, they don't need inoculations, they don't have to learn other peoples' languages, they don't have families, they don't have to send their kids to school, they never require furloughs, they never retire on pensions, and they never die. They go anytime, anywhere, as they're sent. They appear, and men are startled by their appearance and listen to what they say. They don't have an "old Adam." They never get mad nor impatient, either with themselves or with others, but they are always sweet and gentle and winsome. Lord, why didn't you give the job to angels?"

But God has put this treasure in earthen vessels. He's given his work to people—with all their failures and shortcomings and weaknesses. I feel this suggests that a missionary in our day and generation, as in any other, must recognize that fact and learn to live within his limitations.

This problem is a common one to missionaries. In fact, we all have great trouble learning to live within or with our limitations. The best of us have them. There are those who have learned that lesson well, thank God. I think of some of the most triumphant missionaries I have met; whenever one sees them, somehow they just pass on a sort of victory, gladness, and joy, in spite of the fact that they may be crippled or blind or limited in some other way. They've accepted their limitations; they live within them. They turn their attention from these things to Jesus, and looking unto him they are radiant, and their faces are never confounded. The life of God is manifest in their mortal life.

Now when you look closely at the missionary movement, you'll see something of the limitations we struggle with. In Bishop Stephen Neil's book, *"The Unfinished Task,"* we read as follows:

What is the situation of the Church today? We look out on disobedient churches and an unfinished task. What of the past? It can be summed up in two phrases. It is the history of disobedient churches and of unfinished tasks. And yet God has used even those disobedient churches to do great things, and has brought into being a universal Church. Missionaries have on the whole been a feeble folk, not very wise, not very holy, not very patient. They have broken most of the commandments and fallen into every conceivable mistake. And yet God has used their weakness to bring into existence a universal Church. Missionary societies and churches have run their affairs in a way that would have reduced any ordinary business firm to bankruptcy in a year. They have tolerated rivalry, overlapping, waste and imprudence. And yet God has taken them up, with all their follies, into his service for the creation of a universal Church. Converts have been terribly disappointing. Some have lapsed, others have grown arrogant and unusable, the majority have sunk down all too quickly into spiritual mediocrity. And yet, with all their failures, they have been God's front line for the winning of a universal Church. And so it goes on. [1]

Just look at yourself carefully and you'll see something of the nature of that frail, marred, broken, cracked vessel. But God has been pleased to put this treasure in earthen vessels that the glory of his work might be of God and not of men.

## WITH GOOD COURAGE

Finally, I gather from the Apostle Paul that what a missionary in his day needed, and what a missionary today needs, is to learn the secret of how not to lose heart. Paul says, "Therefore being engaged in this service by the mercy of God, we do not lose heart." And verse sixteen, "So we do not lose heart." Chapter five, verse six, "So we are always of good courage." The problems and difficulties that are outside of us, that seem to stop or hinder us, and the problems, tensions, and difficulties that are within our ranks and within our own hearts sometimes threaten us with despair. I would think it strange if those of you whom God appoints as missionaries never taste that despair. There come times when your heart sinks, when courage seems to have fled, when everything turns to darkness for you. In view of the world we face and the task we have to fulfill, one thing we must learn is how to keep courage, how not to lose heart.

Let me underline three points in Paul's own testimony that will encourage us.

1—**By the Mercy of God.** First, he says, "Therefore being engaged in this service by the mercy of God, we do not lose heart." We've not been sent by men, we've been sent by God. And this work God has given to us, he's given to us by his mercy. Even as by his mercy, he accepts woebegone, helpless sinners into his family, so also by his mercy he has made us his servants and ambassadors. The task we have is one God has given to us in his mercy. We have this calling by the mercy of God. There is always hope in the mercy of God. When we turn from ourselves and all that we see around us, to God and to his promises, his Word will hold us, build us up, and strengthen us. For God has given us his work to do, not because we're so smart and clever and able and gifted, but by his mercy. He's put his name upon us, feeble and undeserving though we are, and he sends us forth in his name and by his power. It's all by his mercy! It is when we forget this truth that we run into discouragement.

Stay aware of God's mercy. Live in the glory of it, and it will nourish your heart with courage and with hope and with gladness.

**2—Through Daily Renewal.** Second, in verse 16, "So we do not lose heart. Though our outer nature is wasting away, our inner nature is being renewed every day." Though things may fall apart in our lives or in our ministry or all around us, though difficulties may be so great as to seem insurmountable, still there is for God's servant a daily renewal. It's possible; it is ours unless we fail to appropriate it. Day by day our hearts may be renewed in the joy of our salvation. "Restore unto me the joy of thy salvation," says David, "and uphold me with thy free spirit (with a willing spirit). Then will I teach transgressors thy ways; and sinners shall be converted unto thee." God's man today must experience in his heart the daily renewal of the grace of God and of the power and blessing of the Holy Spirit.

**3—By Faith in the Unseen.** Third, the apostle asserts in verse 17, "This slight momentary affliction is preparing for us an eternal weight of glory beyond all comparison, because we look not to the things that are seen but to the things that are unseen; for the things that are seen are transient, but the things that are unseen are eternal." Here is the third secret for renewed courage. Abraham walked all his days in the certainty of God's promise regarding what was unseen. God said, "I'll give you this land, I'll give you a seed, and I will put upon you my blessing." God made a covenant with him, and he walked in the unseen provisions of that covenant all his days. You'll find this disregard of visible supports over and over again through the Scriptures. You'll see how men of God walked as though seeing him who is invisible—by faith in the unseen resources of the Godhead. Those pilgrims are pictured in chapter eleven of the Book of Hebrews as walking their way through the years, heading for a homeland, looking for a city, greeting it from afar—a city whose builder and maker is God.

This kingdom which had come into their hearts shall one day come in great fullness, with power and great glory. We shall see the triumph of God's grace and power, when with the return of our Savior, he will bring all nations to judgment and establish his righteous rule over all. Knowing this, we set our affections on things that are above where Christ is seated at the right hand of God. So we do not lose heart. Full of courage rather, we move on as the Apostle Paul did day by day in the strength of the Lord, able to say till the end of our lives, "I stand today doing the job God has given me to do."

Let us pray. We thank thee, Lord Jesus Christ, for the treasure thou has given us. We thank thee, too, that thou hast put this treasure into earthen vessels. We thank thee that thou hast taken us up into thy purposes, feeble and faltering as we are. We thank thee that the Holy Spirit has been given to dwell in us and to work within our hearts, both to will and to do thy good pleasure.

Help us to be diligent in our calling. Help us to be earnest about it. Help us to be faithful, not simply at those times when we're called on to do great things, but in the day-by-day detail of our tasks. Help us, dear Lord, to be of good courage and not to faint. Help us in these days, now while we study or work, in the place where we are, to do thy work with a wholehearted faith, with joy and gladness and thanksgiving.

As thou dost lead us step by step to go forward, send us, if it be thy will, into the far places of the world, to join hands with others in the work of thy kingdom. Lord, we pray, make the way plain and grant us the grace and strength to do that work well—to do it for Jesus' sake, that his name may be glorified by us and among us all. Amen

[1] Stephen Neill, *The Unfinished Task* (London: Lutterworth Press, 1957), pp. 221-222.

# 18

# The Missionary Supporter

The story of Elijah in 1 Kings 17:13-16 is a beautiful picture of close fellowship between two believers in obedience to God and missionary service. Elijah is the missionary, and a poor widow is his supporter. For more than a year she supported and cared for him. There are several very helpful things that we may learn from her story.

1—**The work of missions is mutual.** God uses one person to support another. He might have continued to care for the prophet by sending ravens to feed him in the wilderness, but it is his plan that we should work together. It was just as miraculous for the widow to have bread to give to Elijah every day as it was for the ravens to bring him food. And it was pleasing to God that she should trust him every day not only for her own bread, but also for some food to give Elijah.

2— **God works in the darkest days.** His program must go forward in the most evil times, when sin and war and famine are running free in the world. Then if ever he is at work, for "where sin abounded, there did grace abound more exceedingly." So it is not strange even in the darkest times to see him call out missionaries and also those who shall support them.

3—**The supporter is called and appointed to the work of supplying the missionary** as truly as the missionary is called to go and give his time and his life to the work on the field. So the supporter does not give to missions as though he were giving a donation or a gift to a good cause. But he realizes, rather, that he has been commanded to sustain and support some Elijah, just as the widow was. He is not merely making an investment in some worthy project, but he is doing the thing that God has specifically called and equipped him to do.

4—**God very often commands the poor to support his missionary servants.** He could have sent Elijah to Obadiah, who was a well-to-do cabinet minister in the government. But he sent him to this poor woman instead. There is a principle in this. It is the rule in the Kingdom of God. God does not seek the help of the rich and strong. He uses those who are nothing, and who have their backs to the wall. They will have only God to look to, and will be more likely to trust him to enable them to do his will.

5—**What we have is enough for God to use.** All the widow had was a small handful of meal and a few drops of oil, and two sticks for a fire. And that was all that God asked of her. That was enough for his purposes. He blessed it and made it suffice for more than a year. And all that he needs now is just what we have. If we yield it to God for his use, and ourselves along with it, this will be enough for the evangelization of the whole world.

6—**God asked the widow for support that meant sacrifice for her.** It was not easy. It cost her everything. She was poor. She had endured sorrow. She had a dependent child. And yet God said: "Make first a cake for me . . . and then one for yourself." God can only use people who are first of all surrendered to him, and sacrifice is the touchstone of surrender and love.

7—**The real secret of the supporter's ministry is faith.** Save for a promise from Elijah's God, the widow could not have ventured out on such a sacrifice. God did not ask her to give up one world without giving her another in its place. He does not ask us to offer up our worldly means for his service without promising us his divine provision. He never asks for a blind surrender. To an ignorant person it may look foolish for the farmer to throw his good grain into the ground and cover it up, but the harvest rewards his faith. So we give to God and his work in proportion to our confidence in him and his promises.

8—**The widow's obedience was the first step toward a yet deeper experience of God's power and grace.** In our growth in grace we must be willing to be like children, not like vegetables. It takes obedience to grow. It takes venturing faith to grow. It takes responsibility to grow. It takes larger and larger tasks to grow. And the man or woman who obeys God, who ventures out in trust, who constantly assumes bigger responsibilities as he labors with God for the redemption of the world, will really grow. The rest will be like vegetables.

Maybe God is saying to some of us: "GO, FOR I HAVE COMMANDED A WIDOW TO SUSTAIN THEE."

# *19*
# Church Renewal and Mission

*A letter written by Paul to a missionary on April 2, 1970.*

Dear _____,

Perhaps you have noticed it, or perhaps not, but it appears to me that the big "line" that will be taken in the major denominations in the next ten years will be, "the church is the congregation." And if this is true, "then let the congregation be what it truly is—the Church!"

This, it can be seen, is becoming the "front-burner" issue in the thinking and propaganda of the World Council, of Lutheran World Federation, of the National Council of Churches, of the nine-church merger, and now also in the top departments and seminaries of the three big Lutheran church bodies.

The reason for this: New Testament studies show this to be the concept of the Early Church concerning its nature. Hierarchies are falling, papal power is breaking up, unified budgets get weaker, centralized departments of the church cannot find any new ideas, congregations are wanting to do things on their own, pastors are getting tired of being pushers for the church's central office, everyone is weary of trying to meet quotas set by top planners in the headquarter offices. It seems that the free-blown nobodies in the local assemblies have snatched the ball away from the professionals in church administration and are running away with the game in the churches of Latin America and Africa.

The implications of this change are very great: For one thing, the structures and administration of the big church bodies will be affected in a very large measure. Church politics will have quite a different flavor. The big push will not be so much a jostling and pushing for top jobs in the church but an ambition to develop a line and program that congregations will go for and support. Synods cannot give out a budget tax to congregations and ask them to meet it, but will instead have to structure their budgets on the basis of what the congregations decide they want to give.

There will be a loosening up all down the line to allow the congregations their rightful freedom of expression, decision and function. No longer will they be able to harness all the congregations to the same liturgy, the same church school program, the same youth program, the same LCW program, the same confirmation curriculum, or the same song book. There is a widespread reaction against any more of this management and manipulation from the top down upon the congregations.

This means too that there will be many spontaneous movements that will be springing up, all kinds of them . . .

Not all the popes and bishops and presidents and executive secretaries and church editors and board chairmen and pastors are for this, to be sure. But the tide is coming in and I don't think it can be stopped. Better to catch it and ride with it. For I think it comes from the Holy Spirit. There is prayer and talk of RENEWAL—and I think renewal is happening all around.

Three cheers for God—Father, Son and Holy Spirit. To God belongs the victory. Amen!

Yours in His Fellowship,

*P.J.L.*

# 20

# To Belong
# or Not to Belong

*Paul wrote this letter to a missionary in Pakistan in May 1960.*

Dear _____,

Thank you for your letter of May 2, (1960). So good of you to add your personal comments on the back side of the air letter, which had to do with the complex problem of our relationship to the Pakistan Lutheran Church (PLC). This question is full of tension and strain and I feel this very much with all of you. I wish it were possible to settle and resolve it both quickly and easily, but it seems this is not so.

Your letter and a few letters from others there on the field have made it plain and clear that you see no other possible course and that you are bound in conscience to quit the PLC, and our mission too if we continue relations with that church. What seems so clear to you has not yet come to be that clear to me. I have no objection to getting all the light that is available that would lead to this conclusion and my natural sympathies would make me a good candidate for conviction along that line.

I may be mistaken, but I wonder if the problem is not closely related to a very touchy problem we face constantly here in our Lutheran churches in the USA. Right along I get letters from people here and there asking whether or not they should leave their congregation and their synod because of all the wrong things that they see there.

This week a very earnest Christian man in Chicago wrote his second letter to me. He has been a deacon in his church and has been a delegate to conference and synod meetings and has served on some church boards too. He is very greatly troubled and wonders if he should leave his church and synod. He mentioned that other people he knows have come to believe that it is scriptural for them to quit their churches as they cannot remain any longer in such churches and keep a clear conscience before God. This man of course is not a rare case. There are really thousands that are similarly troubled over these same matters. And the answer is not easy to find.

Let me share with you what, in substance, I told this man in Chicago and you may be able to see why the necessity to leave the church in order to keep a good conscience is not as compelling to me as it seems to be to others.

First of all, I agreed with this man that the problems he mentioned are real. The world has invaded the church to a very terrible extent. Many pastors are manifestly unsaved and need to be converted. Modernism has been finding its way in also, more and more, and by our church's association with the National Christian Council and World Christian Council we have opened the way for apostasy and heresy to invite themselves among us too. All of this is no doubt true. And yet, while I deplore these conditions and feel deeply anxious for the future of the church, I do not feel as yet that these conditions should compel me to leave my congregation and synod in order to keep free from indirect involvement, in order to have no part in supporting wrongs, and in order to keep a good conscience before God. Let me try to explain why.

From the earliest days of Christianity there have been two fundamental emphases that have existed side by side when it comes to the doctrine and program of the church. One is the institutional and the other is the sectarian emphasis or viewpoint. Sometimes these have been in strong conflict with each other and sometimes they have appeared in combination.

The institutional view has seen the church primarily as an external organization and has been concerned with organizational continuity—that is with keeping the institutional church going, age after age. This continuity it has tried to insure through a properly and legitimately ordained priesthood, validated by certain external rites and ceremonies which are made uniform all through the church. To be saved it becomes necessary to be subject to the church organization and its constituted leaders. This interpretation is of course seen in its extreme form in the Roman Catholic Church, but it is by no means restricted to it. Wherever an ecclesiastical organization seeks to perpetuate itself for its own sake, wherever membership in the church is equated with participation in the order and program of a particular church organization, there the institutional view is present.

It is not at all accidental then, that the sectarian view has developed as an antithesis to an undue emphasis upon the institutional church. It has come about as a revolt against it, and has maintained that the church is essentially a company composed only of those who are truly Christian. It has then to define what a true Christian really is. Sometimes moral purity is stressed and it is maintained that only those who live a godly life really belong to the church. At other times purity of doctrine has been central, and conformity to a fixed theological standard and creed has been demanded as a minimal requirement for membership in the church. Or again, it has been a combination of both of these prerequisites. Frequently it has been held that the church is the company of the elect, wherever they may be, that they are known only to God.

In all cases, however, there is the idea of a select group, set apart not only from the world but also from false Christians. To the sectarian folks, organizational forms are relatively unimportant, for the church exists only in the mind of God and in the hearts of true "born-again" believers.

It may be that the presence of each of these elements or emphases in extreme form in the history of the Church and of Christian faith indicates that each has sought to preserve an important element of the true doctrine of the church and that each has managed to do so by sacrificing and losing other important elements.

Luther and his followers have criticized both of these lines of emphasis and the Lutheran doctrine of the church developed out of a simultaneous opposition to both. This can be traced in Luther's writings and in the symbolic writings and statements of faith.

If I'm not mistaken, it was in opposition to the Roman Catholic idea of the church as an external organization that Article VII of the Augsburg Confession defined the church as the "Congregation of Saints," and this was developed in much greater detail in the Apology of the Augsburg Confession. The church cannot be merely an external institution, for then its difference from the kingdom of the devil and from the people of the world would not be apparent . . . so in criticizing Roman Catholic institutionalism, Lutheran teachers have employed many of the arguments that serve the sectarian position.

But Luther and those who followed him were just as emphatic in repudiating the sectarian viewpoint. In Article III of the Augsburg Confession, they refused to support in any way the idea of the "pure church" where people refused to acknowledge the validity of the ministry of evil pastors. The sectarian leaders claimed to be carrying out in practice what Luther had been teaching in principle, and to avoid being classified with them in their extreme emphasis Luther was compelled to develop the functional aspect or idea of the church's life. The Lutherans did speak of the church as the "congregation of the saints," but they refused to interpret or define "saints" in the sectarian way. And thus they tried to keep clear of them. This was a very sharp and hot issue of contention during the Reformation.

Lutherans have tried to explain this paradoxical, mid-way-between position in various ways. The doctrine of the visible and invisible church has been one serious attempt to come to terms with it. But perhaps the best figure is the New Testament picture of the Church as the Body of Christ. As a body it has form and structure and is active and perceptible as an organization. But it has a life to it which cannot be seen except by one who is himself alive.

The Church is a body among other bodies in society. As such

it often suffers and partakes of the same ills that befall other bodies and organizations. There can come sores and wounds to this body and it can suffer at the hands of evil men. It can be persecuted, betrayed, arrested and imprisoned. It can be attacked and rent asunder by schisms and distressed by heretics and apostates (as Paul said would happen to the church in Ephesus; see Acts 20:29-30). As with any body, it may carry both living and dead cells, and the distinction is not always clear.

Perhaps this follows upon the traditional situation in the Hebrew nation. They were the chosen and adopted people of God. God dealt with the whole nation as such, and his commands and directions were given to them as a national group, even though not all of the people were in heart the people of God. Paul pointed this out in Romans 2:28, "For he is not a Jew who is one outwardly, nor is true circumcision something external and physical. He is a Jew who is one inwardly, and real circumcision is a matter of the heart, spiritual and not literal." In saying this Paul is putting into his own words what many of the prophets had said long before.

Terrible conditions of evil and wickedness sometimes dominated and ruled in even the most holy and sacred parts of Hebrew life. God took ways to deal with these things, but never did he suggest that the true Jews should separate themselves from the false Jews and form a more pure people of God. God's way with his people was to send times of judgment upon them to cleanse them, and to send prophets to call them to repentance.

With this understanding of the church, many men, godly men with sensitive hearts and consciences, have refused to quit the church because evil things were present, even when they had gotten the upper hand. Indeed, their consciences would have forbidden them to leave. Think of Hauge in Norway, who suffered imprisonment for years at the insistence of church leaders who found this the only way to silence him from preaching the Word of God. But he held his movement within the church and no threat to him would make him budge from this position. Germany has many examples of the same. And in England men were burned at the stake at Smithfield. While they renounced the evils and heresies of Romanism that had taken leadership in the church, they refused to join the sectarian dissenters and quit the church. Some would rather be burned than do that.

One of my favorite authors is J.C. Ryle, Lord Bishop of Liverpool, England. He wrote very extensively and preached unceasingly all through his long ministry. He was the acknowledged leader of the evangelical movement in the Church of England in his day. He wrote, lectured and preached against worldliness, heresy and apostasy in the church and sought by every means he could to bring revival and repentance to the Anglican Church. Sectarians and dissenters flocked to hear him and were greatly stimulated and blessed by his ministry. They continually urged and pleaded with him to ditch the Church of England but he steadfastly refused. His convictions and conscience would never allow him to do that. He vigorously championed the thirty-nine articles of the Anglican Confession and led people to pray for the salvation of the church.

These are some of the things that stick in my mind and explain why I hesitate to reach the conclusion that when sickness and spiritual plagues come in to afflict the church that the time has come to leave it and form another church group where we can by our own control keep clear of and pure from these things.

Now undoubtedly there is a close relation between this problem in our churches as I face it in my mind and the way the Pakistan problem looks to me. I may be quite wrong in associating the one with the other, or seeing any similarity in the situations. And if so, I trust that the Lord will help me to see the difference and not to let my attitude in the one case influence my thinking in the other. And I will appreciate any light that can come upon it. The conscience can be trusted to act upon what is right and to urge and to command what is right. And it can be trusted always to renounce and reject what is wrong. But the conscience cannot decide what is right and wrong. This insight about the rightness and wrongness of this must be arrived at by a careful application of the Bible to situations, by prayerful reflection, by helpful discussion and fellowship, by gathering up as much knowledge of the facts as we can, and above all by the witness of the Holy Spirit "who shall guide you into all the truth."

May the peace of the Lord be with you and guard your heart and thoughts in Christ Jesus.

Yours in His Fellowship,

*Paul J. Lindell*

# 21

# Bare Feet
# on a Mud Floor

## How To Do Evangelism and Church Planting

*A letter to a World Mission Prayer League missionary in Bolivia, May 1951.*

Dear _____,

The Bolivian field is really a very promising field. The Indians are considered by observers to be among the most responsive people you can find anywhere. Others who have worked among them or their Andean relatives in Chile, Peru or Ecuador have found them to be so and have a considerable harvest to show for their efforts. If after twelve years of labor with quite a considerable staff we have so very little to show for it, I think that there must be some reason for it. The reason is not to be found in any lack of consecration among the workers, nor in any spiritual delinquency. What is needed is not so much the power of an unusual revival as it is the need for some better system and plan and program in the work and thus to harness better the power we do have. The Pentecostals and Quakers both seem to know how to do this better than we do.

We have been weak in: (1) throwing out the net, (2) drawing in the net, (3) organizing the catch.

1—**Throwing out the net.** Intensive evangelism. John Carlson did this for six months in La Paz until at the end of the time there was quite a body of people who were coming regularly to the chapel. He preached and fished all day long like a barker at the fair. The suggestion that the field be worked over by a team with a tent for preaching, teaching and organizing is good. This plan is exactly what my father did in China and many congregations sprang up as a result.

2—**Drawing in the net.** Use all the nationals you can for this. In a local campaign enlist every willing person to get out and bring in the people. Especially the believers. This is the style in the Korean Church. The believers are out every Sunday afternoon to round up the people of the city to come to the Sunday night meetings. There is no substitute for getting people to pitch in and help. And the Indians know this. They do this in their village work, or in putting new roofs on their houses. Such a plan is in their system already and can be nicely directed to this useful task. Give them all jobs to do in the campaign.

At the meetings get people to sign, so to speak, on the line. There are various ways of doing this. Get their names, put them on a chart like in Sunday school, and get them to come every day at a certain time for class instruction in the faith. If your hold on them is vague and indefinite they will soon slip away. But if they have registered interest and want instruction, then you have a toehold on them. It is certainly imperative to use some nationals on your team. Never mind aiming at any certain number. Take the first one you can get and start with him. Then take the next one too. In due time you will see how many you can handle. Train them in the course of campaigning, systematically, with orderly lessons.

3—**Organizing the catch.** First, it is important to rope in the *inquiring unbeliever*. The old missionaries called them "catechumens." In China we called them "inquirers." I have suggested in the previous paragraph the importance of this. It is easiest to hold them if you organize them into definite classes for instruction. It is important to get them started with the idea of membership in something. Therefore, enroll them in a class of inquirers and make them cover systematically the course of study and instruction which shall lead them to a good and saving knowledge of the gospel and prepare them for membership in the church when they are ready.

Finally, it is important to organize the *believers*. A clear and definite pattern should be cast for developing the organization and membership of a congregation. Qualifications for membership should be made clear. The essential factors which go to make a congregation should likewise be clear and workable. A congregation should be organized at the very earliest opportunity. Until it is organized the sense of responsibility is hazy. Once it is organized the membership has assumed definite responsibilities and obligations. It may be necessary to do this a step at a time, but not to do so is fatal. Transfer responsibility and authority to a small committee maybe to start with; with the missionary as adviser. There is likely a native pattern which is used by the Indians in their local community organization which could be used with much effectiveness in the organization of the church. A definite membership roll is essential.

See that the group has a duly appointed leader or pastor — part time or full time; part pay or full pay, as they are able to bear it. Have them get their own place of worship. If they want to use the mission chapel as a place to assemble the congregation then let them pay rent for it just as they would if they rented a room down the street. The separation of mission from church must be clear. The mission is exotic, impermanent and may soon be moved away. The church is permanent and must therefore get on its own feet, even if it is in bare feet on a mud floor.

*Paul Lindell*